WRITING A JOB-WINNING RÉSUMÉ

by
John E. McLaughlin &
Stephen K. Merman

A SPECTRUM BOOK

PRENTICE-HALL, INC. / ENGLEWOOD CLIFFS, NEW JERSEY 07632

Library of Congress Cataloging in Publication Data

McLaughlin, John E.
   Writing a job-winning résumé.

   (A Spectrum Book)
   Includes index.
   1. Résumé (Employment)   I. Merman, Stephen K.,
joint author.   II. Title
HF5383.M23   650.1′4   80-11475
ISBN 0-13-970236-9
ISBN 0-13-970228-8 (pbk.)

A SPECTRUM BOOK

Printed in the United States of America

17   16   15   14   13

Prentice-Hall International, Inc., *London*
Prentice-Hall of Australia Pty. Limited, *Sydney*
Prentice-Hall of Canada, Ltd., *Toronto*
Prentice-Hall of India Private Limited, *New Delhi*
Prentice-Hall of Japan, Inc., *Tokyo*
Prentice-Hall of Southeast Asia Pte. Ltd., *Singapore*
Whitehall Books Limited, *Wellington, New Zealand*

TO:

All people who seek higher levels of career achievement and success and who recognize the importance of the resume as a career planning and self-marketing strategy.

Contents

10 *Case Studies and Sample Resumes*

Take a Look at
What Others Have Done, 82

11 *How to Lay Out, Edit, Type, Copy, Select Paper*

Do Not Fold,
Spindle, or Mutilate, 124

About This Book

THE RESUME EXPERIENCE

What! Another resume book? Another "format" to fit my life into? Another way to be different?

WRITING A JOB WINNING RESUME

Not at all. Writing a *Job-Winning Resume* is for ambitious job and career strategists who view the successful management of their career as a *total experience!*

For them, this book is important and an integral part of that experience.

We were determined not to write "just another resume book," and we set out to make it possible for you to write a job-winning resume in just a *single evening.* So, when you complete this book, you will have completed your resume—it's that simple!

Numerous examples and exercises are provided, making the "whys" and "how-tos" of writing resumes clearer and easier for you to duplicate.

In addition, you will actually experience the rationale behind each example via the Case Study approach in Chapter 10. There is even a section on how to layout your resume—whether to have it typed, copied or printed—and there are tips on paper selection. Chapter 12 goes "Beyond the Resume Experience" and includes unusual and unique resumes.

The main point is: Creating a resume, one that works for *you*, does not need to be an agonizing, time-consuming, frustrating chore. It can be an easy step-by-step process—thought-provoking, insightful, and interesting. In short, it can be a positive career development experience, and we call it "The Resume Experience."

So relax, select a quiet time, and get ready to "get into" writing a job-winning resume!

CREATIVE WAYS TO UNCOVER JOB LEADS

To share their experience in personal career development and job search strategies, authors John E. McLaughlin and Stephen K. Merman determined to take their book one step further and discuss ways you can *use* your resume to win a good job. This facet of The Resume Experience is in Part II, "Now That You've Got It, What Are You Going to Do With It?"

ACTION LETTERS THAT GET JOBS

As a special bonus, the authors have included a complete section of Action Letters to help you uncover job leads. These action letter samples cover four main areas: Job Lead Development Letters, Thank You and Interview Follow-Up Letters, Creating and Maintaining Influential Contacts, and finally, Corporation/Organizational Research Letters.

A WORD OF THANKS

The creation of any publication requires the personal sacrifice of not only the authors but of several others intimately involved with them. We wish to extend our appreciation to all our friends who invested time and energy to help create a practical and useful resume writing resource.

A special affection is extended to our families, Mickey, Kim, and Kevin Merman, and Cindy, Kristie and Matt McLaughlin.

JOHN E. MCLAUGHLIN
STEPHEN K. MERMAN

What is written without effort is, in general, read without pleasure.
—**Samuel Johnson**

The engravings throughout this book are reproduced from
The Early Illustrators and *Attention Getting Old Engravings,*
both published by the Art Direction Book Company of New York.

Spend an Evening with the Resume Experience

Introduction

"Time you enjoy wasting is not time wasted."
—Anonymous

WHAT IS THE RESUME EXPERIENCE?

Experiences are often perceived as either **positive or negative.** Writing a resume is a negative experience for most of us. We would like to help you change that negative experience to a *positive* one.

It's You! **The Resume Experience** is a positive statement about **yourself,** an advertisement to help **you** get the job **you** want. Your resume is your product literature, public relations, and salesperson all wrapped up in one package. It is often the only thing representing *you* in the organization prior to or following an interview. In fact, your resume can even become a person:

Sam: Well, it's between these two people.

Cheryl: Let me see those resumes again. Uh huh. They both look pretty qualified, you know, this person seems more together, well-rounded, has a sense of direction and comes across more dynamically. What do you think?

Sam: You know, you're right! That's good input from just looking at a resume. You've helped me make up my mind!

The Good Things Now that's an example of creating a *positive* statement about yourself, which can result in positive experiences for you. In short, The Resume Experience shows yourself (and others) *the positive you.*

Too often, our society focuses on the negative aspects of our "selves" and the positive aspects are left unrecognized or out of focus. Therefore, the first step in writing a resume is to get people to eliminate the negatives, to focus on the positives, and to express their uniqueness on paper.

Feeling good about yourself is the underlying theme of The Resume Experience. It's a neat feeling, the idea that *you can do it,* that you are a skilled person and that you have the capability to contribute!

So, from this point on, we give you permission to state good things about yourself. It's okay—you will not be criticized for believing in *yourself.* Thus, The Resume Experience is:

* Experiencing **yourself** as *an organized person!* Seeing your life and career organized on two sheets of paper is a positive experience!

   * Experiencing **yourself** as *a growing professional!* Seeing yourself as a growing and dynamic professional is a positive experience!

      * Experiencing **yourself** as *a unique person* is a positive experience!

* Experiencing **yourself** on *a career path!* Seeing where you are in relation to your life and career plan is a positive experience!

* Experiencing **yourself** as being *in control!* Seeing yourself in control by choosing your own direction and making choices is a positive experience!

* Experiencing **yourself** as a person *committed to goals*—personal, social, and professional goals—is a positive experience!

What Is An Evening with The Resume Experience Worth?

Question: Hey! So far so good! I've never looked at resumes in that way before; but what other results can I expect from having a well-written resume?

Answer: Plenty! Here are just six results of creating a dynamic and creative resume:

The Right Job   *Getting A Job That Fits You Personally, Socially, and Professionally.* Most of us, in our work lives, will spend 45 years and over 90,000 hours doing our jobs! With this amount of time invested, getting the right job is crucial.

Some of us will try to fit a square peg into a round hole and become frustrated; others will play Don Quixote and chase unrealistic dreams and windmills.

Some are like the race horse who runs frantically, but without direction. They don't get anywhere because they don't really know where they're going. Others are like the tortoise who secretly longs to be a race horse. They don't realize the value of being themselves, of being the best person they **can** be.

Fortunately, some of us will eagerly go to work, looking forward to the challenges of the job and interaction with peers. Since getting a job that fits you is important for life and career satisfaction, your resume should reflect realistically what that job should be.

Plus: *Job Satisfaction.* If a job fits you personally, socially, and professionally, it has a great chance of providing job satisfaction. Being happy in your work will have a positive effect on your relationships with others.

Job Ecology. The ability to create and maintain a satisfying job environment is a skill few people have. From a well-prepared resume, you can predict your job environment.

Job ecology relates to selecting all aspects of the job—the people you will be working with, your activities, the decor of the work place, and the relationships you create with co-workers.

Physical and Mental Well-Being. Creating a positive statement about oneself can be healthy for an individual. Dissatisfaction, frustration, feelings of worthlessness, or a feeling of "just marking time" can cost each of us a great deal in time, money, and energy.

The *creative* resume can help you regroup, help you to start feeling good about yourself again!

Identify Employment Barriers. Don't let mountains *keep* you from success! It is amazing how people create ways to keep themselves from getting satisfying and rewarding jobs. **That's right,** they keep themselves miserable by creating and maintaining mental barriers to employment.

Such as: * too many job changes
         * age
            * too big
               * too little
                  * male
                     * female
                       * or whatever!

Don't!   People create these employment barriers, which often are **assumptions.** Many of us have experienced people who have kept themselves from a job opportunity because they **assumed** they were too old, needed a degree, or were overweight. The problem is that these barriers are reflected in the resume!

By completing your resume you identify these barriers and work to minimize or completely eliminate them, so they no longer block your path to job and career success.

Financial Well-Being. Want to improve your financial status? The well-prepared resume will start you on the road to gaining financial freedom. The document will open doors and generate interviews, as well as increasing your visibility for better jobs.

What Not To Worry About At This Time!

Functional? Chronological? French fold? Objectives? One page? Two pages? Centered? Off-centered? Typeset? Offset? Photograph? No photograph? First person? Third person? Cover letter? Action verbs? Summary of qualifications?

There are an incredible number of options, opinions, and formats on "how to write a resume." No wonder many people are confused and professional resume writers do a flourishing business!

The first section of The Resume Experience concentrates on *you* and all those things, events, activities, and situations that have made *the you that exists at this moment*. This is an information-gathering section, so don't be concerned about the incredible number of options, opinions, and formats. Put them out of your mind so they won't confuse and frustrate your early efforts.

Warming Up To The Resume Experience

Getting ready for The Resume Experience is an experience in itself! We feel that the creation of this document is so important and vital for your career development that we want you to spend a few moments focusing your energies and attention on the activity revolving around writing a resume.

Getting Ready: Here are some tips:

* Select a work environment where you will be relaxed and comfortable, with a minimum amount of distraction.
  * Plan to spend four to six hours.
    * Gather all the materials we recommend at the end of this section so you won't be interrupted by having to locate them.
      * Get comfortable—whatever that means to you!

Relax For those of you who are adventurous and need additional warm-up, the following relaxation technique may help:

* Close your eyes. Breathe deeply and steadily for several minutes.
  * Sit up straight in a chair with your feet flat on the floor. This helps get oxygen to the brain.
    * Slowly—very slowly—begin rotating your head as far forward as possible, then to the side, then as far back as possible, then to the side, and repeat the motion.

This activity loosens the neck muscles and helps you relax.

You're a   Another way to get into the experience:
Success!

* Close your eyes and actually visualize the completed resume.

   * It looks well-organized, neat, and professional.

     * You feel good about it because it represents you in different and unique ways.

       * Try fantasizing a job interview, with the interviewer reading your resume and asking you questions from it!

Finally, put yourself in a positive mood—create a positive feeling about you and your background. You need to uncover the positive aspects of your life, the events you feel good about. Think about this; then complete the "I Am" Activity in Figure I-1, designed to bring out these positive aspects.

Figure I-1. The "I Am" Activity.

Directions: On a separate sheet of paper, complete the sentence below with as many *positive* statements about yourself as possible. Try to list at least 20 statements.
"I am . . .

Illustrations: Here are some examples of what others have said about themselves:

"I am: creative
     a good wife/husband
     a good student
     good at organizing
     an effective parent
     a good lover
     effective at human relations
     an effective administrator
     an efficient craftsman
     a skilled artist
     a good volunteer
     a writer
     efficient with details
     unique
     able to judge others accurately
     able to solve complicated mathematical problems
     a good neighbor
     a good listener
     a good driver
     an effective presenter to large groups"

Feeling better? We hope so!

Tools of the Trade

As with any creation, you must have the necessary tools. Collecting these resources before you start will minimize interruptions. In many cases, these resources will actually stimulate your creativeness and contribute to your uniqueness.

Have On Hand:

*Paper, pens, or pencils, rulers, marking pens, scissors

* Dictionary

  * Thesaurus

    * Old employment records

      * School records (formal and non-formal learning experiences)

        * Any research on the industry or organization where you plan to focus your job search.

          * A job description of the position you desire (if known or available)

            * Business cards or address books for references

* Information on all associations or professional organizations

  * Awards, citations, plaques, recognition certificates

    * Previous and current appointment schedule books

      * Any other documents or sources which describe what you have done and where you did it

        * Notes or records of any self-assessment activities

Begin!

You are now ready to begin The Resume Experience. So roll up your sleeves, get comfortable and let's go!

1

The Top of
the Page
Component
#1

Heading and Identification

WHAT KIND OF HEADING?

What do we call this thing we are creating? You name it, and it has probably been tried!

To some extent its title depends on your status as a job seeker. If you are recently out of school and are looking for your first job in the "real world," the time-tested, generally accepted French word *RESUME* will suffice. This word simply means "a summary," "a condensed statement," or "a short history."

This term is most commonly used by those *not* in executive, supervisory, or technical positions. However, when it *is* used, it should be centered at the top of the page with spaces between each letter:

R E S U M E

The following heading (a bit of flourish) is usually employed by executives, managers/supervisors, technically oriented people (engineers, data processors, and so on), or other professional persons. It can be centered at the top of the page

PROFESSIONAL PROFILE

or, an accepted business format is to put the heading at the top left-hand side of the page (block style), as in

PROFESSIONAL PROFILE

If currently employed, it is proper to add the word **"Confidential,"** especially if you would like to stay employed during your job search.

Identify It!   CONFIDENTIAL PROFESSIONAL PROFILE

The important point is that you include a heading of some kind on your resume so the reader knows what he or she is reading!

NAME, ADDRESS, AND TELEPHONE NUMBER

What's In A Name?

Our names can often cause problems on resumes! Some of us have very common names while others have lengthy or difficult names.

For various reasons, we have adopted nicknames which feel comfortable to us but are potential problems on resumes. Names with sexual overtones or names that have been shortened from original names may come across as "cute" and "unprofessional."

Take the case of Richard Horatio Peters:

> Well, I was always hassled in school but it's not that big of a problem now.
>
> I make sure that people know me as Richard H. Peters. I feel it is more professional than Dick Peters or R. H. Peters.
>
> I use Richard H. Peters on all correspondence and, of course, on my resume.

Middle names often create images when used with the first name. Should this happen, initials may be used instead of the full name.

A Pro!   *The key point is:* You want your name to appear as professional as possible without creating any negative images or reactions.

Don't!   In addition, a nickname should not be used along with your regular name, "Henry (Hank) T. Smith, for example." Also, the use of surnames such as "junior," "senior," "IV," and so on should be dropped. Although you may prefer these names as a way of personally identifying you, they can create adverse images and reactions when used on a resume!

Spell It Out   **Address**

The address is located below the name and is typed or printed in lower case letters. It is best to avoid the use of abbreviations to minimize confusion as to your exact location. *Be sure to include the zip code!*

Telephone Number

Nothing is more frustrating for an employer than a phone number that's *always busy* or one that is not answered despite repeated attempts! We can only speculate as to how many job opportunities are lost because the telephone number listed is not covered or out of service, or because the person answering does not know the party asked for! So:

* List a telephone number where you can be *easily reached!*
  * List *a back-up number* just in case the first is unattended.
    * During an active job-search, *make sure these phones will be answered.*

Pivotal: Always list your Area Code such as:

```
Business Telephone: (415) 752-2118
```

If you are *unemployed,* not at home, or conducting a confidential job search, you may want to investigate the use of *an answering service.*

CONFIDENTIAL SEARCH

When an employer discovers the fact that an employee is looking for another job, the employee's desire to leave is either tolerated and accepted or considered cause for immediate termination. Generally, government, education, and the social services fields view job hunting as normal employee behavior. Industry and business, on the other hand, view this activity as disloyalty (as "mentally quitting a job") and react negatively.

Remind Them!   You must *be careful.* Should you choose to include "Confidential" as part of your resume heading, be certain to indicate this important point to all those contacted. *Don't assume* that a prospective employer understands this just from reading your resume.

EXAMPLES AND ILLUSTRATIONS

The following examples of various headings are recommended for your resume (Similarities to actual names, addresses, and telephone numbers throughout *Writing a Job-Winning Resume* is purely coincidental!):

```
RESUME

HENRY T. SMITH
918 South Lindenberry Court
Chicago, Illinois  61820

Home Telephone: (312) 345-5643
Business Telephone: (312) 686-9908
```

RESUME

HENRY T. SMITH
918 South Lindenberry Court
Chicago, Illinois 61820

Home Telephone: (312) 345-5643
Business Telephone: (312) 686-9908

PROFESSIONAL PROFILE

HENRY T. SMITH
918 South Lindenberry Court
Chicago, Illinois 61820

Home Telephone: (312) 345-5643
Business Telephone: (312) 686-9908

PROFESSIONAL PROFILE

HENRY T. SMITH
918 South Lindenberry Court
Chicago, Illinois 61820

Home Telephone: (312) 345-5643
Business Telephone: (312) 686-9908

CONFIDENTIAL

PROFESSIONAL PROFILE

HENRY T. SMITH
918 South Lindenberry Court
Chicago, Illinois 61820

Home Telephone: (312) 345-5643
Business Telephone: (312) 686-9908

PROBLEMS
AND SOLUTIONS

Long-Distance Job Search

Circulating your resume long distance can create communication problems. The question is: Whom will the employer call first—you or one of the local applicants?

To avoid being screened out, you may want to subscribe to a local *post office box number,* plus list a local *answering service* on your resume.

The impression is that you are in the area, so make certain to answer all messages promptly and schedule interviews at times when you plan to be in that area.

No Business Telephone?

If you choose not to list your business telephone number, or if you are currently unemployed and unavailable to answer your telephone, the best solution is an *answering service.*

The investment is *well worth* the money. The benefits are satisfied employers who are able to reach you easily plus complete coverage of all potential job opportunities!

Moving or Relocating?

Moving or relocating is a very common situation in our highly mobile society. Various solutions are:

* An answering service and post office box in the city or town where you are moving

   * An answering service in the city or town where you are leaving

      * List the telephone number and address of a friend or associate who will agree to take messages

         * Acquire an address or telephone number before you relocate and indicate on the resume that the number will be in effect on a certain date

You are now ready for Resume Action Step #1.

15   THE TOP OF THE PAGE

RESUME ACTION STEP #1

Objective: To *write* Component #1, Heading and Identification, for *your* resume.

Materials: Pencil and paper

Action Step: Following the guidelines indicated in this chapter, *write* the *Heading and Identification* component for your resume on a piece of paper.

For additional examples and illustrations, refer to Chapter 10, "Case Studies."

When you have completed this component, put your paper aside and move on to the next component, Chapter 2. You will have an opportunity to put it all together later!

2

Be Objective About Your Objective

Component #2

Career/Job Objective

—Rebellion against your handicaps gets you nowhere ...
Self-pity gets you nowhere ...

One must have the adventurous daring to accept oneself
as a bundle of possibilities and undertake the most
interesting game in the world ...

making the most of one's best.
—Harry Emerson Fosdick

THE CAREER/JOB OBJECTIVE

One of the more controversial components of a resume is the inclusion of a **Career Objective** or a **Job Goal.** Of the many professional resume writers, some argue for and some against the inclusion of a career or job objective. Some include only a **Career Objective,** some just a **Job Objective,** while others do not include it under any circumstances! We feel it is a matter of style—*your style!* We view it is an important component and would like to go on record as recommending it for *any* resume.

You again!
Also, it's important not to get hung up on the choice of term—either "objective" or "goal." Again it's a matter of style and what you feel comfortable using!

Definition:
We view the **Career Objective** as a long-term commitment and the **Job Goal** as short-term commitment which will eventually contribute to reaching a career objective; however, using the terms interchangeably is acceptable!

For Example:
The *Job Goal* can refer to a general job position, such as "a position in general management" or to a specific job such as "a senior programmer/analyst."

Question: I like the idea of stating Career or Job Objective to help clarify my direction, but what are some other advantages?

Answer: The career or job objective does several positive things for a dynamic resume:

* First, it illustrates that the person has *direction*—on a growing and dynamic career path.

   * Second, it demonstrates to an employer that you are a person who has done *serious thinking* about your life and career, a person who knows what you *WANT* and can *communicate* it clearly and positively!

      * Third, it allows you to tailor your resume to *specific* job opportunities.

         * Fourth, it is an *action statement* representing you as an "action person"—alive, vital, and eager to contribute.

Idea!
You can redo the resume with each job opening and create a dynamic resume which fits a particular job opening. This strategy can be impressive to a potential employer!

Careful!
A word of caution: In order to create an effective and realistic career/job objective—one with **impact**—you must do some thinking about yourself: *Who* are you? Where do you want to go? Why? This will not only aid you in preparing your resume but will also contribute to your effectiveness during a job interview.

Stating The Career/Job Objective In Action Terms

Sell Yourself

The resume is often viewed as an advertisement, a brochure that sells a product; that product is you! Your best approach is to put **sell** into the resume.

Marketing experts highly recommend the use of words and statements designed to motivate the buyer to *take action*—in this case to arrange an interview!

Question: Well, I don't know about this. I don't feel very comfortable with the idea of tooting my own horn or bragging the way a Madison Avenue ad agency would do. I don't see myself as a huckster! So what do I do?

Answer: Well, there are two key points to consider: First of all, "being yourself" is important; however, you must also be aware that the resume is your marketing tool. Action statements can be toned down to make them acceptable to you and yet retain their marketing qualities.

Secondly, you should be proud of your skills, abilities, and professionalism. If you have made significant contributions and accomplishments in your life and career, then you should feel comfortable in stating them in positive and meaningful ways.

The Idea Is: Create a positive image of yourself so that the employer *wants* to have an interview with you. Don't allow society to put down The Positive You. Remember, you were given permission to state The Positive You on a resume!

Illustrations and Examples of Objectives

Let the following guidelines and examples of Career Objectives and Job Goals guide you in developing your objectives in Resume Action Step #2:

* To make the career objective realistic, ask yourself the question "Can I actually *attain* it?"

    * Does the career objective have *meaning* for you? You must feel *comfortable* with the words used. They must express precisely *what you want to do.*

        * Write the career objective so that you can *express* it and *support* it in a job interview.

* Career objectives are created with "action verbs." The writer must imply an *action*. For example, during your career, you see yourself *doing* something, like "supervising" or "researching" or "consulting."

   * The **career objective,** then, is an action statement which tells the reader what you see yourself doing in the *future*.

Important!   Here are examples of Career Objectives:

```
    To consult with human resource de-
velopment personnel in medium to large
organizations with a special emphasis
on communication and secretarial train-
ing.
```

The Action Verb in this example is "consult."

```
    To administer a large recreation-
al or amusement park, including plan-
ning, marketing, and programming
functions.
```

The Action Verb in this example is "administer"; there are also other action terms such as "planning" "marketing" and "programming."

```
    To administer programs in higher edu-
cation and to teach post-secondary
courses in history, sociology, and an-
thropology.
```

There are two Action Verbs in this objective—"administer" and "teach."

A Clear Objective   These examples are broad and cover a wide range of skills. They are **action-oriented** and provide more than one Career Objective in one sentence. An employer has little doubt as to what these persons want to *do!*

The statements aren't vague, such as "I wish I could be a ..." or "Someday I want to ..." or "I would eventually like to develop my skill in. ... " Rather, they *specifically* state what the person sees himself/herself doing!

Examples of Job Goals. Following are listed additional examples of Career Objectives with corresponding Job Goals. It's your choice—the broad **Career Objective** or the short-range **Job Goal.** You may even wish to list both, with the Career Objective listed first. A word of caution: If you list both, be certain that the Job Goal fits the Career Objective, because the Job Goal represents a step in your career which will eventually lead to your Career Objective. AGAIN, this component shows you have direction and indicates that you are *planning* your career to make significant contributions to the organization and yourself!

Careful!
An Exception

In short, if your ultimate career objective is completely "out of tune" with your immediate job goal, do not list both; list only the Job Goal. (Employers will be suspicious if your Career Objective is completely different from the job opening.) Once you have examined the following examples of Job Goals, you are ready for Resume Action Step #2:

```
Career Objective: To consult with human
   resource development personnel in me-
   dium to large organizations with a spe-
   cial emphasis on communication and
   secretarial training.

Job Goal: To be an internal consultant
   for the Human Resource Development
   Office at XYZ Corporation.
```

```
Career Objective: To administer a me-
   dium to large continuing education
   program for an urban university and
   to develop innovative learning sys-
   tems for adult learners.

Job Goal: To be a program specialist
   for the Center for Continuing Educa-
   tion at State Urban University.
```

Career Objective: To administer a marketing program for a small to medium size manufacturing firm to include design and implementation of marketing strategies, planning, budgeting, and evaluation.

Job Goal: To be a territorial sales representative for a medium size manufacturing firm.

RESUME ACTION STEP # 2

Objective: To write Component # 2, the Career/Job Objective for *your* resume.

Materials: Pencil and paper

Action Step: Following the guidelines in this chapter, *write* the Career or Job Objective for your resume on a separate sheet of paper.

Remember, the objective is written in two parts—the *Action Verb* plus the *Action Objective.*

The **Action Verb** is what you see yourself *doing* (that is, planning, managing, marketing, administering, preparing, and so on).

The **Action Objective** describes the *who, what,* or *where* of the action.

Design your work paper in the following fashion:

```
                ACTION VERB                        ACTION STATEMENT

   To _____                  _____

                                                _____

                                                _____



   Completed Career Objective: _____

   _____

   _____

   Completed Job Goal: _____

   _____
```

For additional examples and illustrations, refer to Chapter 10, "Case Studies."
Note: There are additional examples of Action Verbs in Chapter Three.

When you have completed this component put your paper aside and move on to the next component, Chapter 3. You will have an opportunity to put it all together later!

3

Hey! Look at Me!
Component #3

What we have done is the only mirror by which we can see what we are.
—Thomas Carlyle

Experience: Summary of Qualifications: Accomplishments

Once again, putting together a convincing advertisement for yourself is a creative and rewarding experience. A *positive self-image* results in a *dynamic resume,* which creates a *positive* image in the mind of the employer!

The "Experience Paragraph," the "Summary of Qualifications," or "Accomplishments" component allows you the unique option to create an effective and dynamic resume. This section can say more about the *"real* you" and provides the opportunity to express your skills in more creative ways than in any other section of the resume.

USING ACTION VERBS

Just as you wrote a Career/Job Objective using Action Verbs, you should also incorporate Action Terms into Component #3. In this section, they are used primarily to *begin* an action statement in order to draw attention to a positive statement. Consider the following examples:

```
Proven ability to work independently,
provide leadership, and work well with
people at all levels of an organization.

Motivated to do a job well and make a
significant bottom line contribution.

Created a marketing program which re-
sulted in rapid market penetration of
a new consumer goods product resulting
in 165% of quota.

Successfully managed a large profession-
al association for three years resulting
in a 50% increase in membership and a
stabilized financial situation.
```

Make An Impact!   These statements combine action-oriented terms with accomplishments and results. They are impressive, dynamic and have a significant **impact** on the reader. In short, they create a positive image of the person! Use the following list of Action Verbs to create a powerful, action-oriented statement about you:

Action Verbs	approved	created	developed
	implemented	planned	indexed
	composed	directed	administered
	controlled	revised	distributed
	initiated	investigated	analyzed
	coordinated	negotiated	determined
	supervised	expanded	presided
	trained	assembled	governed
	facilitated	persuaded	arranged
	organized	recruited	invented
	moderated	presented	designed
	managed	sorted	evaluated
	solved	researched	diagnosed

RESUME ACTION STATEMENTS

The following is an example of turning a "ho-hum" resume statement into an Action Statement which adds _dynamism_ to your resume. Adding action verbs and phrases which imply motion, success, and strong leadership gets the employer's attention. The ho-hum resume statement:

```
Responsibilities included supervision,
marketing, budgeting, and promotion.
```

The Action-oriented Resume Statement:

```
*Recommended and implemented a 10% staff
 reduction in my department with no loss
 in performance.
```

```
*Implemented a controversial new market-
 ing program which resulted in a 45% in-
 crease in sales bringing the plant to
 90% operating efficiency.
```

```
*Designed a publicity campaign which re-
 sulted in company feature articles ap-
 pearing in two prominent national peri-
 odicals.
```

These are statements of **concrete results** which clearly tell the employer that these persons have been in situations where they contributed to improve the profit picture and the efficiency of the organization.

A WORD ABOUT RESUME DESIGN

The design of a resume can contribute greatly to the dynamics you are creating. Proper spacing, correct margins, and plenty of "white space" allows for easy readibility of your resume. The use of *asterisks* or a *period* preceding a list of action statements can draw attention to your qualifications and accomplishments. Simple, short, brief statements that are *to the point* will provide just the right touch for a resume, making an impact on the reader. Resume design is discussed in greater detail in Chapter 11.

HOW TO SELECT THE "EXPERIENCE," "SUMMARY OF QUALIFICATIONS," OR "ACCOMPLISHMENTS" HEADING FOR COMPONENT #3.

In designing this component, you have the option of labeling it either "Experience," "Summary of Qualifications," or "Accomplishments."

In some cases, you may desire to combine Experience with Accomplishments or Summary of Qualifications with Accomplishments. Some may argue that *accomplishments* are the same as *qualifications.* However, examples given later in this chapter will illustrate the possible combinations. The following is a guideline for selection:

* The beginning job-seeker who is "short on experience" should use the Summary of Qualifications heading to highlight life and human relations skills, as well as youth group and school accomplishments.

   * The job-seeker who has a great deal of experience in the same field but with several organizations may select the Experience paragraph to stress the highlights of his or her skill areas. This could be followed by a section on significant accomplishments.

      * Writing the Experience paragraph then eliminates the need for repeating responsibilities in the Work History component (Chapter 4).

         * A person with an extensive list of accomplishments may select to list this section only. Accomplishments can also be listed as part of the Work History component.

The primary reasons for selecting one of the headings are: **Which markets you best** and which is the most comfortable for you!

Experientially Speaking

The Experience paragraph is one of the most difficult sections to create because you are required to summarize your experience in one to four well-written paragraphs!

Everything Counts

Question: Why is this section just called Experience? Why not call it "Work Experience"?

Answer: The purpose of this section is to encourage you to include *life experiences* as well as *work experiences* in the description of your skills and abilities!

Further, it has been a common misunderstanding that if a skill wasn't learned or applied in an on-the-job setting (a full-time, salaried position) then it isn't a developed skill!

Career development specialists now know that this notion is nonsense! We are able to learn a variety of work-related skills through everyday living.

The fact that a housewife can *inventory* household goods, and a high-school student can *coordinate* and *organize* a school dance, demonstrates the fact that we do learn skills in places other than formal work settings! Therefore the concept of **transferable skills** means that a skill learned and applied in one setting can also be applied in another setting.

Managing and promoting a program for a volunteer organization requires the same skills needed to manage and promote a program in business and industry. Consequently the Experience paragraph lends itself to the inclusion of experiences learned and gained from *life* as well as *work*. Your writing objective becomes the task of making visible your best skills as they relate to your career or job objective. A second task is to make it clear, precise, positive, and to avoid repetition. Each paragraph should summarize a skill that relates to the job opening. The most relevant skills are discussed first, followed by related skill areas.

Rewrite it!

Once this section is completed, we recommend you put it aside and review it later. Constant rewriting sharpens this component to a point where it becomes a creative and unique statement of your skills. Remember: This section will be the most widely read among prospective employers. *It must be well-done!* It must include evidence of learned skills, success, responsibilities, accomplishments, and problems you helped solve. In short, it must portray you as a growing person seeking opportunities that will contribute to that growth! An illustrative Experience paragraph is as follows:

CAREER OBJECTIVE: To administer the training program for a large industrial organization and to use my skills in communication, leadership, and adult learning in the design and implementation of educational programs.

EXPERIENCE:

*Designed, developed, and implemented training programs for business and industry in sales and supervisory training, career development, and executive development for a major urban university.

*Designed and implemented a leadership program that resulted in the training of over 600 executives in organizations in a major metropolitan area.

*Taught, administered, and programmed continuing education courses, including: credit and non-credit workshops, seminars, and conferences for business, industry, and government.

*Skilled in the area of public relations and communications and have developed positive working relationships with many types of organizations.

In this illustration all the skill areas are related to the Career Objective. The most important skill areas are indicated **first.** There is no mention of any organization or location where the person received the experience. That information appears later in the resume. Finally, note how an accomplishment was integrated with the skill area in the second paragraph.

Summary of Qualifications

Some resumes read like a company employment application—vital statistics and cold, hard, data. There is very little human quality to a job application, very little opportunity to express who you really are!

Present a Person

The purpose of the Summary of Qualifications section is to allow creative job-seekers to present themselves as *individuals* able to work, communicate, and relate well with people.

Question: What are some of the advantages of the Summary of Qualifications section compared to the Experience paragraph?

Answer: Both are excellent components. However, one advantage is that the Summary of Qualifications *maximizes* an individual's positive qualifications and *minimizes* any employment barriers which may exist in other parts of the resume, such as too many jobs, not enough experience, age, or lack of degree!

Numerous examples of the Summary of Qualifications are listed in the Case Study Section, Chapter 10. Here is one example:

SUMMARY OF QUALIFICATIONS:

```
*Proven ability to work with clients,
 the public, and professional associa-
 tions.

*Have directly supervised the work ac-
 tivities of others.

*Have been completely responsible for
 evaluating organizational training
 programs.

*Am considered by others to be
 dependable, creative, and a problem
 solver.
```

Remember:

This section can be integrated with the Accomplishments related to your work life. In addition, they can be skills or abilities derived from your activities with schools, churches, volunteer groups, or everyday life interactions!

As you recall, we provided a list of action verbs that could be utilized to create a powerful, action-oriented statement about you.

Now we are taking the same list, changing a few endings, adding a few verbs, and deriving a skill-area list from which you can draw terms to describe your qualifications, experience, and accomplishments. The skill words are:

Skill Verbs	observing	inspecting	examining
	diagnosing	deciding	determining
	evaluating	judging	imagining
	inventing	idea formulation	creating
	designing	creative thinking	developing
	coordinating	controlling	risk taking
	initiating	organizing	leading
	managing	directing	calculating
	figuring	interviewing	consulting
	servicing	planning	researching
	analyzing	facilitating	writing
	systematizing	reading	speaking

Accomplishments—Look At Those Trophies!

Unfortunately, society does not always encourage openly discussing our accomplishments, but with The Resume Experience you have that opportunity! No one is going to toot your horn for you. Remember, the competition for *good* jobs is fierce.

Speak Up!　　Accomplishments can stand alone or be integrated with the other two sections. It's simply a matter of choice.

The key point is: list accomplishments that generally resulted in some event or situation which those around you viewed very positively and which you felt very good about.

Identify Them!　　So, you need to identify accomplishments which had an *impact* on an organization or a group of people, clearly stating that they benefited because of your accomplishment!

The following are examples of accomplishments often found in creative resumes; which illustrate how an accomplishment statement can be created to stand alone or combine with either the Experience or Summary of Qualifications sections.

```
*As a result of conducting a statistical
 study, implemented a program that re-
 duced inventory costs by $180,000 per
 year.
```

```
*Implemented a needs analysis and train-
 ing program that reduced equipment down
 time and changeover by 24%

*Consistently performed at 150% of quota
 in a three state sales territory for 12
 consecutive quarters.

*Initiated a membership update system
 that reduced return mail by 30% for a
 major volunteer organization.
```

To assist in formulating accomplishment statements, the following questions will jog your memory:

* List specific instances when you saved your organization money.

  * List specific instances when you increased sales, exceeded quotas, successfully
    introduced a new product, or developed a new marketing strategy.

    * List instances when you more effectively and efficiently utilized staff or
      people or reorganized for staff reduction.

      * List any ideas that you submitted to a group or organization and
        that were adopted by them.

        * List any large projects in which you provided the leadership
          or had responsibility.

          * List any procedures, policies, or programs that under
            your leadership were significant and successful or solved
            a problem.

            * List any and all accomplishments, regardless of their
              impact. The only criterion is that they felt good and
              you felt more *confident* about yourself as a result.

You are now ready for Resume Action Step #3.

When you have completed this component, put your paper
aside and move on to the next component, Chapter 4. You will
have an opportunity to put it all together later.

RESUME ACTION STEP # 3

Objective: To *write* an Experience paragraph, a Summary of Qualifications, and an Accomplishment section for your resume.
Note: We recommend writing all three sections even if you plan to use only one on your final resume. Writing all three will give you the option of combining statements that highlight you best.

Materials: Pencil and paper
Past and current work records
Old resumes
Information which will assist you in recalling facts about your experience.

Action Step: Following the guidelines in this chapter, *write* the Experience paragraph, the Summary of Qualifications, and Accomplishments section on a separate piece of paper.
On a separate sheet of paper, lay out the following headings:
Experience Paragraph:

Summary of Qualifications:
Accomplishments:

For additional examples and illustration, refer to Chapter 10, "Case Studies."

Follow-up: Following the creation of this section, you may want to put it aside and review it in a few days. This may generate additional ideas.

Also, a good strategy is to have a friend or associate read the section and get his/her reaction.

4

Hey! Look Where I've Been!
Component #4

Work Experience

The start a young person makes counts most of all.
In baseball they do not lavish the highest praise on the players who reach second or third . . .
But on those who have the ability to get to first.
No one can steal first!
—Anonymous

While most of us have a work history, for some of us the experience was good, for others not so good.

Listing your work experience correctly and clearly is an important resume strategy. Dates of employment, titles, and locations of the organization are all part of this component.

LET'S LOOK AT THE BASICS!

Your Organization

Many organizations are listed or registered under one name but do business under other names! Use the abbreviation "DBA" for the phrase "doing business as." For example:

Dextra Incorporated DBA Hoop Industries

Unless there is some reason for being obscure about the name of your organization, be sure to list it correctly.

Spell It Out   If your organization is a component of a larger entity, be sure to list it that way. For example:

Commercial Credit Corporation, a Division of Control Data

Avoid the use of abbreviations wherever possible!

The Location

Your resume should look organized and uncluttered; therefore we recommend you omit the complete street address of an organization where you were employed. Simply indicate your city and state; if more is required, it will be because you have a real job opportunity and you can supply the addresses during an interview.

Your Title

Be Brief   Your position title can appear in a variety of unique and creative ways. Right now, however, the title should appear accurately and honestly. For example, if you are a "secretary" but your job duties are those of an "administrative assistant," then you should list "secretary." You must be careful. Consider the case of Cynthia:

Well, I felt it was time to change jobs, for a number of reasons. So I completed my resume and listed my job title as "administrative assistant." My official title, however, was "secretary" to the principal of a high school, but I had actually been administrating the entire school for my employer for several years. I really felt I was an administrative assistant! Boy! Was I shocked when my boss insisted that my title be listed as "secretary" and that was what he was going to say to anyone who inquired about my position. Well there was nothing else to do. I had to change the job classification on my resume back to "secretary."

Not all cases are as grim as Cynthia's. Many have been able to creatively overstate their job titles and springboard themselves to greater responsibilities and success.

Be Correct
Be Creative
There are creative ways to say "secretary," such as "executive secretary," or "administrative secretary."

A Word of
Caution
Whatever title is listed, make certain it's comfortable for you and that it will be supported by your former employer!

Dates of Employment

Be Honest
Regarding dates of employment, it's best to *honestly* list both the months and years of employment. Our experience is that most resume readers are wise to applicants who list only years of employment as a strategy to conceal gaps in employment.

But for most of us there *are* brief gaps in employment. If it's only a matter of thirty days or so, the creative resume writer may consider tightening up the dates by stretching an ending or a beginning date of employment to cover the gap. The following is an illustration of how The Basics appear on a resume:

```
WORK HISTORY:

August, 1974 to Present       Refinery Engineer, Offshore
                              Oil Company, Houston, Texas

March, 1970 to August,        Engineering Technician,
   1974                       Pipeline Fabrication Company,
                              Tulsa, Oklahoma

February, 1969 to            Materials Lab Technician,
   March, 1970               Pipeline Fabrication Company,
                              Tulsa, Oklahoma
```

December, 1967 to	Metal Fabrication Shop Worker
February, 1969	Metal Fabricators, Incorporated
	Tulsa, Oklahoma

Note that months and years were cited, and there were no addresses or abbreviations. Also, the positions are listed in chronological order beginning with the *most recent*.

A LITTLE BIT OF PUFFERY OR THE THESAURUS IS NOT AN EXTINCT DINOSAUR

Say It Better   Now that you understand the basics of the Work Experience component, let's look at creative ways to make this section *lively and dynamic*. Word selection and word patterns—depending on your use of them—can make significant contributions to your resume. We have already discussed the use of *Action* terms; now we want you to discover better ways to say what you mean. Here's where the Thesaurus and our old friend the Dictionary come in.

To begin our creative look at this component we introduce two concepts: *The Job Description* and *The Organization Description*.

The Job Description

Most job or position descriptions are good bedtime reading—they put you to sleep! Perhaps they are meant to be that way to create confusion as to precisely *what* the person is supposed to be doing in the organization. The Job Description, however, can be used in the Work History component in brief, concise, and creative ways. By using a Thesaurus you can select other words with the same meaning as the words used in the job description. For example, instead of writing "responsibilities included" you might use "accountable for" as a variation.

In describing a job many people lose creativity by having a laundry list of duties but not writing about what they actually did! Here is a guideline describing the important elements which you include in your Job Description:

* Include words about abilities, skills, and problem-solving activities used to fulfill the job duties.
  * Avoid always beginning a statement with "Responsibilities included . . . ."
    * Indicate accomplishments related to the position wherever possible.
      * Use Action Terms.
        * Select words that represent you as a person concerned with a career path and upward mobility—a person "on the move."
          * The description of your most recent job should be the most thorough and detailed, unless it was a short-term experience.
            * Select words to indicate your relationship to other people within the organization, such as: "Vice President of Marketing reporting directly to the Chief Executive Officer."

In the following illustration of a creatively written job description for a resume, the writer indicates an accomplishment that enhanced the job description considerably.

```
August, 1972 to May, 1974   THARCO PROPERTIES, INCORPORATED
                            Chicago, Illinois,
                            Assistant General Manager

            Initially was in charge of the total field
            administrative function. Due to the very
            rapid growth of the firm (17 properties to
            over 100 in less than two years), my
            responsibilities evolved into those of sales,
            marketing, public relations, and advertising.
```

The Organization Description

A unique variation within the Work Experience component is a brief description of what your organization does. This description helps the reader to better understand your position, because it's in relation to the role of the organization. (In some cases—such as educational institutions, social services, or volunteer organizations—the purpose of the organization is obvious, and to make statements about its purpose only clutters the resume.)

Here is a simple, brief illustration of combining the Organization Description with the Position Description that states the general nature and purposes of the organization:

```
May, 1974 to Present      GENERAL PROPERTIES, INCORPORATED
                          Chicago, Illinois

          General Manager

          General Properties, Incorporated is involved
          in the real estate investment and property
          management field.

          Have total fiduciary responsibilities as
          well as the overall management responsibilities
          of the personnel function, accounting, legal,
          supervision of over 40 people, field administra-
          tion, and maintenance.
```

A PARTING SHOT ABOUT TITLES

In designing the Work Experience component, job titles can be handled in a variety of ways. One format is to double space the title and place it directly below the organization's name; then double space again to begin the description.

```
For Example:  HOOK INDUSTRIES, INC./Saint Louis, Missouri

          This position as Assistant Production
          Manager reported directly to the
          Production Manager and consisted of...
```

Or

An alternative format is to include your title in the first paragraph of the position description, as in:

```
HOOK INDUSTRIES, INC./Saint Louis, Missouri

This position as Assistant Production
Manager reported directly to the
Production Manager and consisted of...
```

Question: I've seen cases where there is no title, only a job description. What is recommended in these cases?

Answer: You're right. Some positions do not have titles. The best approach in these cases is to begin with the job responsibilities and include some indication of the general position within the organization, as in:

```
This position in the sales department
reported to the Department Manager
and included responsibilities as...
```

PROBLEMS AND SOLUTIONS

The following are common problems confronting resume writers in creating the Work History component:

How Far Back?   *Question:* I'm 42 years old. Do I have to list my jobs going all the way back to my high school years?

Answer: The accepted rule of thumb is to list jobs for the past ten years. If the last ten years have been with the same organization then it is acceptable to list two or three previous positions; however, be sure to list any promotions within an organization. In addition, any work experience prior to ten years can be summarized as "Early Work History," providing it is relevant to the job or career objective.

Include Everything?   *Question:* I'm a beginning job seeker. In high school and college I must have held at least twenty different jobs. How do I handle that?

Answer: Working and going to school is not easy; in fact, it's admirable. A listing of some of the jobs is appropriate, particularly if they involved skills and abilities related to your Job Goal or Career Objective.

Select and Summarize   Select those positions where you had problem-solving responsibilities and made accomplishments. The remainder can be grouped in a summary paragraph beginning with the words

"While attending school fulltime, I held a variety of part-time positions which included . . . ."

Unemployment?   *Question:*   There have been occasions when I was unemployed. In one instance, I was traveling with my family, while another time, I was doing research and writing. These gaps in my Work History won't look good on my resume. What should I do?

         Answer: The listing of your work history does not have to consist of formal, salaried, "punch-the-clock" situations. Periods spent on your own—traveling, studying, or just finding yourself—can be represented in the Work History section.

The Key Is: Use a "little bit of puffery" in describing these experiences. Describe them as learning experiences that contributed to your personal and professional growth. The research experience could be described as follows:

```
Spent six months operating on a tight
schedule to organize and analyze
research and statistical data for a
major research grant.
```

Bad Health?   *Question:*   That is an interesting way to handle gaps in employment. My situation is different in that I was out of work for a year and two months with a severe health problem! How do I say *that* on a resume!

         Answer: The key here is to create a statement that is *neutral*—one that doesn't suggest anything positive or negative. Simply list the inclusive dates, then state "Leave of Absence" which could mean anything. This tells the employer nothing about the "nature" of the leave and provides the opportunity to relate your health problem in a very positive way during a job interview. In short, a neutral statement allows you to turn a potential negative on the resume into a positive—in person! During the interview, express the health problem as an opportunity to read, take courses, catch up on current events, and improve relationships with your family. Because of your leave of absence you are a much better person, and a better professional to hire.

Make It a Plus   *Question:*   I have had too many jobs, especially during the last five years; a couple of them lasted only a few months! I doubt if any of my previous employers would give me a reference. Is there a creative way to handle that on a resume?

Answer: A difficult problem indeed! Our experience has indicated that many persons with this problem will write in as much *growth* and *increased responsibility* as they can, for each successive job. They create the sequence of jobs in such a way that *every change was a chance* to move up or improve their professionalism!

Other solutions are possible. Eliminate the short-term jobs, stretch the dates a bit, and provide continuity to the work history. Or present yourself as an *"internal consultant"* working for a variety of organizations. Be certain that you have the approval of those organizations to list it that way, as in the case of Charles Wood:

Boy! Did I bounce around! It seemed like one year I just couldn't get a handle on keeping a job. But being in adult education and program development, I felt I could come up with a better solution to this problem on my resume.

So I went to my previous employers and told them about my dilemma. I requested that I be allowed to list my short stay with them as an internal consulting position. They *agreed!* It really helped the appearance of my resume and it led to my current position.

This part of Charley's resume appeared as:

```
June, 1976 - July, 1977

    As internal consultant, coordinated
    several projects for major univer-
    sities that included . . .
```

You are now ready for Resume Action Step #4. Once you've completed this step, you have completed the component. Put your papers aside and move on to the next component, Chapter 5. You will have an opportunity to put it all together later.

R E S U M E   A C T I O N   S T E P   #4

Objective:	To *write* Component #4, Work Experience, for your resume.
Materials:	Pencil and paper Old job records Previous resumes Copies of previous employment applications Other documents that will assist you in completing this section.
Action Step One:	On a separate sheet of paper, complete the following questions for jobs you have held.

Remember: If your work history goes beyond ten years, that information can be summarized on your resume.

It is important, however, that you get in touch with all of your work experiences—be thorough and creative.

1. What is the *name* of the organization?
2. What is the *location* of the organization?
3. What was your *job title (s)*?
4. What were the *dates of employment*?
5. What *skills and abilities* did you use?
6. What were your *accomplishments* while in the job?
7. What *personal or professional* growth did you experience while on the job?

Action Step Two: For those wishing to summarize odd jobs, temporary employment, or previous work history, refer to the questions posed in Action Step One and write a Summary on a separate sheet of paper.

Action Step Three: Take the information from Steps One and Two and following the guidelines in this chapter, write the Work Experience component on a separate sheet of paper.

For additional examples and illustrations refer to Chapter 10, "Case Studies."

5

Making Cents Out of Education
Component #5

Education

One of the great differences
between the amateur and the
professional is that the latter
has the capacity to progress.
—**W. Somerset Maugham**

The Education component of your resume is designed to give information and facts regarding your *Formal* and *Nonformal* educational experiences. In keeping with the theme of The Resume Experience, statements of educational experiences reflect "the professional you." These experiences may be drawn from several aspects of your life and include learning opportunities from a variety of places.

Question: Is that what you mean when you say "nonformal" education?

Answer: Yes. **Nonformal educational experiences** are those in which you've participated, that have had little structure, and that have provided no formal recognition of your participation.

Examples are:

* Any on-the-job training you may have received
  * Volunteer organization activities
    * Church-related activities
      * Skills acquired by learning a job yourself
        * Filling in for a co-worker who was absent for one reason or another.

These experiences are *life* situations and although they may seem inappropriate for a resume, they still represent times in your life when you acquired job-related skills.

THE HALLOWED HALLS OF IVY

The following information regarding formal educational experiences is considered basic:

Formal   *Name of Institution.* The name of the institution or organization where the learning experience occurred should be indicated on the resume. Again, avoid the use of abbreviations and be certain to include the entire name.

Location of Institution. The exact address of the institution or organization is not important. We recommend listing just the city and state.

Degree, Diploma, or Certificate? What indication do you have of completing the formal educational experience? It is often a piece of paper called a degree, diploma, or certificate. Whatever evidence you have, indicate it on the resume to tell the reader that you not only attended the experience but you *successfully* completed it!

Major Area (s) of Study. The Education section tells the reader your major areas of study during the formal educational experience. Usually, it is appropriate to indicate two or three major areas of study resulting from a formal educational experience.

Career Objective

This section is particularly important if the major areas of study relate to the Career Objective.

EDUCATIONAL EXPERIENCES OF ANOTHER KIND

Experience is usually what you get when you were expecting something else.
—Anonymous

Write It All Down!

The listing of nonformal educational experiences, for purposes of the resume, can include a VARIETY of activities— seminars, continuing education courses, workshops, or courses related to the career objective, are all important. In addition, any on-the-job training activities or special training programs offered by previous employers could be listed as long as they are *related* to the Career Objective.

Keep It Current

If your educational background is weak or dated, then you may want to list any current nonformal experiences that reflect you as interested in personal and professional growth. By the way, seeking out these experiences is important, as they can have impact when listed on your resume.

Nonformal

* The Experience: What was it (on-the-job training, observation, or what)?
  * The Sponsor: The name and location of the organization or activity.
    * When and Where: Dates, city and state.
      * The Benefits: What results did you experience in the way of skill development, personal growth, or new knowledge.

Illustrations and Examples

The following are illustrations of the Education component of a resume. Additional examples are in the Case Study Section, Chapter 10.

EDUCATION: Masters in Public Administration,
              1979, University of Denver,
              Denver, Colorado. Major: Person-
              nel Administration and Human
              Resource Development

              Bachelor of Arts Degree, 1976,
              University of Cincinnati, Cin-
              cinnati, Ohio. Major: Political
              Science. Graduated with honors,
              Deans List, 1975

              Seminar: "Financial Administration
              in the Public Sector," 1977,
              University of Colorado at Denver,
              Denver, Colorado

              Seminar: "Affirmative Action Prog-
              rams," April, 1976, American M
              Management Association, Dallas,
              Texas

EDUCATION: Diploma, 1976, Heritage High School,
              Chicago, Illinois

              Seminar: "Supervising the Volunteer,"
              May, 1977, United Way, Chicago,
              Illinois

              Certificate: Supervisory Management
              Development," 1977, University
              of Utah, Salt Lake City, Utah

              On-The-Job Training, Computerized
              Inventory Control Procedures,
              July, 1977, DACON Incorporated
              Chicago, Illinois

Problems and Solutions

The following are common problems confronting resume writers in creating the Education Component:

Question: I'm 37 years old and have my masters degree. Just how relevant are my high school experiences? Should I list them on my resume?

Answer: Good question! It is acceptable to omit your high school experiences if you possess college or advanced degrees. You're right, there is a point where your high school education ceases to be relevant, but be sure to include it if you don't have a college degree.

Future Graduation Dates. A typical problem facing college students or other adult students returning to school for further education is that they are enrolled in a program but have not yet finished it!

Most people feel uncomfortable in listing a degree or certificate that is not quite theirs!

In Process! The accepted practice is to list the degree and then add the words "in progress" ... or ... "anticipated graduation." This indicates that you are in the process of improving your professionalism by seeking further education and that you are industrious (working fulltime *and* going to school). So, the solution is to list the degree as follows:

```
EDUCATION:  Bachelors Degree in Business Admin-
            istration, Anticipated Graduation,
            1980, University of Kansas, Law-
            rence, Kansas. Majors: Accounting
            and Finance
```

Too Much Education. Believe it or not, some people list too much education on their resumes. With several degrees and considerable training they list every detail; as a result they are viewed as "over-educated" and threatening to an organization.

Cut down on the amount of education listed and list only those experiences relevant to the Career Objective or Job Goal! If you hold a Ph.D. in biology and are seeking a position in sales or management, then don't list the Ph.D., but stress the courses you have taken in sales and management! Remember:

You are not writing your life history in a resume, but a

summary of the most important aspects that relate to what you want to do.

No High-School Diploma! Consider the following case study:

Joe, a 22-year-old retail clerk, had considerable problems staying in school. For some reason, the school's objectives and his were never the same, and he soon dropped out to join the Navy.

Any type of training program soured Joe, and therefore he was never able to adapt to a learning environment.

In his work life Joe was a super salesman. He was skilled in talking with people and could surpass all sales quotas. However, when he tried to advance he discovered that he was considered unqualified because he didn't have a diploma. He wanted a management position badly enough to consider additional education.

Lack of education is clearly a barrier to Joe's advancement into management. On his resume, he had to *maximize* his sales skills and *minimize* the impact of not having a degree. His solution was to enroll in a special college program for adults, which accepted him without a high-school diploma but required acceptable scores on an admission test. So, Joe's Education component looked like this:

EDUCATION: Bachelor of Arts Degree, In Progress, State University, Des Moines, Iowa. Major: General Business.

On-The-Job Training, Point of Purchase Displays, November, 1978, Retail Sales, Incorporated, Des Moines, Iowa.

Stress Skills   If you are a full- or part-time student currently enrolled in an educational program, you can indicate an educational goal. If, however, you have no high-school diploma and no alternatives, then you may consider eliminating the section altogether!

The important point is:

The absence of an Education component means you must compensate for the lack of education by stressing other components of your resume that emphasizes skills and other accomplishments.

Getting More Education. With the increasing importance of adult education, training, and development, it is difficult for a person to avoid participating in some kind of educational program! Almost all universities, colleges, and educational agencies conduct noncredit educational programs for the residents in their areas.

More and more, organizations both private and public, and professional associations, are offering programs for personal and professional enhancement.

The serious career strategist is constantly in search of ways to improve skills and pursue personal development. Programs for self-improvement can usually be related to career and job objectives on your resume.

Now you are ready for RESUME ACTION STEP #5. Once you have completed it, you have finished this component. Put your paper aside and move on to the next component, Chapter 6. You will have an opportunity to put it all together later.

R E S U M E   A C T I O N   S T E P   #5

Objective: To *write* Component #5, Education, for your resume.

Materials: Pencil and paper
Copies of certificates, diplomas, degrees
Enrollment records
Previous daily or weekly planning books
Any documents, records, or information to jog your memory regarding educational experiences.

Action Step: On a separate paper, complete the following questions for each educational experience you have participated in.

Remember: consider *Formal* as well as *Nonformal* experiences and be certain to list *all* of them regardless of whether they are related to your Career Objective. You can eliminate the unrelated information later.

1. List all degrees, diplomas, or certificates using the following column headings:

Degree, Diploma, Certificate	Where	When	Who

2. List all Nonformal educational experiences using the following column headings:

Title of Experience	Where	When	Who

3. Following the guidelines of this chapter, *WRITE* the Education component for your resume.

For additional examples and illustrations refer to Chapter 10, "Case Studies."

6

The Icing on the Cake
Component #6

Related Professional Experience

A wise man will make more opportunities than he finds.
—Francis Bacon

MORE ABOUT YOU

Not everyone can list substantial related professional experience; however, some people have considerable experience *outside* their careers and regular job duties. The Related Professional Experience component presents an opportunity to reflect experience gained from managing or directing volunteer activities, church-related activities, associations, professional societies, or hobbies that require special skills. This component also presents an opportunity to represent any awards, honors, or other forms of recognition you have received. In short, this resume component is an opportunity to tell more about yourself—to brag a bit—and to add credibility to your resume.

What are the Basics?

Which Ones?   *Awards, Accomplishments, Honors, Related Skills.* The following question is the most important guideline in determining which awards, honors, accomplishments, or special skills from outside activities to include in your resume. Ask yourself: Is this **related** to my Career or Job Objective? For example, if you are applying for a government position, do *not include* an award for an editorial you wrote that criticized America's involvement in world affairs; similarly, the fact that you are skilled in floral arranging has little to do with your management skills and would be out of place on your resume. The important point to remember is:

Don't!   Do not include *everything,* just information that enhances your qualifications for a specific job or career.

Professional Associations   You should include any memberships in professional associations and a description of your role in them; this information can greatly enhance your resume. If you are a member of a professional group, you should indicate what the group is and how you participate. In some cases, you may want to include special awards or accomplishments you have achieved as a member. Associations should appear on the resume as follows:

```
RELATED PROFESSIONAL EXPERIENCE:

        American Psychological Association,
           member, 1975 to Present.

        American Humanistic Psychology
           Association, member, 1973 to 1977.
           President, 1975-1976.
```

Or RELATED PROFESSIONAL EXPERIENCE:

National Civil Engineering Society,
member, 1965 to Present

President, 1971-72
Secretary, 1967-68
Treasurer, 1969-70

Students: Students should consider the value of using professional associations. You should become "student members," get active, and include your membership on your resume. This activity demonstrates to a prospective employer that you have a strong desire to participate in the profession and to keep up to date with professional peers, activities, and events.

Any Publications? Most persons who publish are associated with educational or professional organizations and require special

consideration for publications on a resume. Faculty *vitas,* for example, often list pages and pages of publications and research activities.

The Guide   If you have published, listing publications in the Related Professional Experience component is appropriate; however, the same rule applies—Only list a publication if it relates to the career or job objective. A word of caution: Don't overdo it! This section can become lengthy, particularly if you have done a lot of writing.

ILLUSTRATIONS AND EXAMPLES

Here are some illustrations of this component:

RELATED PROFESSIONAL
EXPERIENCE:

Member, Sales and Marketing Executives, Chicago, Illinois, 1975 to Present

Member, American Management Association 1973 to Present

RELATED PROFESSIONAL
EXPERIENCE:

Scholarship, Koch Corporation, University of Houston. Dean's List, 1969

Supervised and assisted in teaching an introductory chemical engineering class, University of Houston, 1972-73

Tutored engineering students in college mathematics and chemistry plus assisted in college preparatory courses for high school students, 1973-74

If you are short on Related Professional Experience but have been recognized for special contributions or awards, you may wish to label this component "Special Awards or Recognition." Note the following illustration:

SPECIAL AWARDS OR RECOGNITION:	*Received recognition for publishing: "Managers and Time Management," <u>Personnel Magazine</u>, November, 1978
	*President, Metro Chapter of Data Processing Managers, 1978-79
	*Recipient, 1977 Woman of the Year Award, League of Women Voters, Saint Louis, Missouri
	*Leadership Award, Baxter Corporation for participation in the Community Fund Drive
	*Volunteer teacher, Valley Junior College, Data Processing, Little Town, Missouri

GETTING INVOLVED.

Question: I know that achievements are measures of success, initiative, and leadership and that I should represent myself as an involved person. But where do I go to join, how do I find the time, and which ones do I join?

Join!   *Answer:*   Glad you asked that! People often fail to get involved because they don't realize the many and varied opportunities available to them as members of professional associations. The best strategy is to seek out one or two professional associations that fit you and your career aspirations and join them! Find out what you've been missing! (You can make time for professional activities—just commit yourself to spending a certain number of hours each month with professional associations and people.)

Changing Jobs?

Finally, if you are a career changer, the professional association provides an unstructured and open environment where you can rap with other professionals. It's an excellent way to become visible and learn about potential careers!

Now you are ready for Resume Action Step #6. When you have completed this component, put your papers aside and move on to the next component, Chapter 7. You will have an opportunity to put it all together later.

R E S U M E   A C T I O N   S T E P   #6

Objective: To *write* Component #6, Related Professional Experience for your resume.

Materials: Pencil and paper
Previous resumes
Documents detailing recognitions, awards, etc.

Action Step: On a separate sheet of paper, *complete* the following questions for each of the Experiences in your background which relate to your Career or Job Objective.
List as many as possible—you can eliminate some later.
1. Name of each experience.
2. Date of each experience
3. Organization offering experience or giving the award or recognition.
4. List any and all affiliations with professional organizations.
5. List any offices held in professional organizations.
6. List any publications
7. List all civic awards and recognition.
8. List all humanitarian awards and recognition.

Following the guidelines in this chapter, *write* the Related Professional Experience component for your resume.

For additional examples and illustrations refer to Chapter 10, "Case Studies."

7

Psst!
Let's Get Personal.
Component #7

Personal Information

Discrimination Exists Despite the Equal Employment Opportunity Act, Affirmative Action Programs, Supreme Court Decisions, and other signs of change, prejudice and discrimination are still a real problem in the interview and hiring practices of *some* organizations. Illustrations of this type of attitude are the following behind-the-scenes comments:

Examples: "Aw, she's young and married. If we hire her, spend time and money in training her, she'll eventually get pregnant and leave us."

"Are you kidding me? At his age, he just isn't going to have the old zip and enthusiasm that a young buck would have. We need young blood in here!"

"Since she's a single parent, I see all kinds of problems—no overtime, running to doctors all the time, no travel. No way!"

"I wouldn't hire *anyone* who is a member of *that* party!"

"Hey! Wait a minute! They can't do that—not in the twentieth century!" We hear you; however, discrimination is a fact of life—it is reality. "They" aren't supposed to do it, but some do!

BARRIERS TO EMPLOYMENT

Personal information on a resume can be a serious problem, because for some of us it sets up a barrier to employment. On the other hand, eliminating this section may create serious doubts on the part of employers—they may wonder what you are hiding.

Barriers to employment are factors that might cause an employer to not hire you. Regardless of the fact that there may be legalities involved, often the personal bias of the employer counts. A number of barriers have already been discussed, such as no experience, too many jobs, gaps in employment, too much education, or being overqualified. Potential barriers in the Personal component are:

* age
   * sex
      * health
         * marital status
           * personal interests

Options: As in other parts of the resume . . . these barriers must be *minimized to eliminate any personal biases* which could exist in the mind of the employer! It is important to remember that you want to omit certain information that could be misinterpreted, to alter your approach with a letter/resume (see Chapter 9), or to eliminate the Personal section altogether.

Our recommendation is to include a Personal component in your resume; its omission can create suspicion. Besides, the Personal component portrays you as a well-rounded individual with interests other than just professional growth.

Making Spring Boards Out of Barriers

Common listings for the Personal Information component are birthdate, marital status, health, and interests. Let's look at them one at a time.

Birthdate/Age. Like other parts of the resume, there is a controversy as to whether Age or Birthdate should be indicated. A person with a young, "marketable age" may prefer to state "AGE—29," while an older person may elect to play down the age by indicating a birthdate such as "BIRTHDATE: May 5, 1934."

The Solution   Our recommendation is: Most persons, regardless of age, should use the Birthdate rather than Age, because your birthdate remains the same while your age changes every year. This approach minimizes age, which can be a barrier in almost every situation!

Marital Status. With the many options in lifestyles these days, it can be difficult to indicate your personal relationships on a resume. Regarding marital status, our position is that you are either Married or you are Single.

If you are Married and choose to indicate it on the resume, it should appear as "MARITAL STATUS: Married." And if you are Single, it should appear as "MARITAL STATUS: Single."

Be Positive!   The Point is: Avoid using terms such as "divorced," "separated," "previously married," or "single parent." These terms can create negative reactions among employers and keep you from getting an interview where you can explain and defend your personal situation. For example, "single parent" on your resume might eliminate you from the running because the employer assumes that you can't travel, that you might have to take time off to handle "kid problems," or that you couldn't work long or odd hours, which may be a condition of employment! So, by stating either Single or Married you leave the option open for an interview where you can state *in positive terms* the special conditions regarding your personal relationships.

Health. There is only *one* way to state your health condition on a resume and that is: "HEALTH: Excellent." If you can't say "excellent" then don't list Health in the Personal component. Unlike Age or Marital Status, your health status usually does not create suspicion if unlisted. Finally, if your health is not good you should practice ways to minimize its impact during a job interview.

Caution: *Interests*. Tennis Anyone? The All-American woman or man often has the image of being well-rounded, "outdoorsie," and an avid tennis player. Watch out for potential barriers in listing Interests. On the plus side, interests can represent you as a well-rounded person, with outside activities and an interest in "keeping fit" and being physically and mentally "active." This component can also represent you as a person concerned about your health, which is an important consideration in hiring an older person. In addition, biases lurk out there among resume readers. For example:

INTERESTS: Tennis, hiking, reading, and duck hunting.

Employer: Duck Hunting?! How could any civilized person shoot ducks! We don't want a person around here who *murders* ducks!

The employer may not understand that most duck hunters are conservationists at heart and actually contribute to preserving ducks rather than pursuing the bloodthirsty elimination of the species.

Rule of Thumb: The safest course is to list only those interests that are acceptable and noncontroversial. If you have "questionable" interests, then *leave them off!* After all, why create unnecessary barriers? Remember: You don't have to list *everything* about yourself—keep it short and simple!

ILLUSTRATIONS AND EXAMPLES

The resume format for Personal Information should appear as follows:

```
PERSONAL INFORMATION: Birthdate: May 5, 1955

                      Marital Status: Married

                      Interests: Golf, Tennis, Physical
                                 Fitness, Reading
```

Or

PERSONAL INFORMATION: Age: 32   Marital Status: Single

Health: Excellent

Interests: Refinishing furniture, reading, art, jogging

You are now ready to complete Resume Action Step #7.

R E S U M E   A C T I O N   S T E P   #7

Objective: To *write* Component #7, Personal Information for your resume.

Materials: Pencil and paper

Action Step: Following the guidelines in this Chapter, *write* the Personal Information component for your resume.

For additional examples and illustrations of layout and design, refer to the Case Study Section in Chapter 10.

When you have completed this component, put your paper aside and move on to the next component, Chapter 8. You will have an opportunity to put it all together later.

8

With Friends Like You, Who Needs Enemies?

Component #8

References

*If everybody remembered the past
nobody would ever forgive anybody.*
—Robert Lynd

HOW TO ENSURE A GOOD REFERENCE

Remember: The question of References usually comes up when the job search is coming down to the wire. When the organization asks for References, you know they are *seriously* considering you but need additional convincing. Unless you have really botched things with a previous employer or other relationship, most references won't knowingly torpedo your new opportunity. The point to learn is:

If you do get tripped up by a reference it is because you didn't cover all your bases.

Question: What do you mean by that? I can't *force* anyone to say good things about me.

Answer: Very simple before you list or offer a reference, you should talk to that reference to establish an understanding. Why? By updating your background with the reference and covering your *good points* and *successes,* you create a partner to help *sell* you to the employer. Secondly, by discussing an opportunity in an enthusiastic and positive way with a previous employer, one who may give you an unfavorable reference, you can *control* the response he or she gives. For instance:

Job-seeker: Well, that's about it, Mr. Simms. I know we have had our differences, but I wanted to let you know that someone may be calling, and I would appreciate a good reference. I really am excited about this job, and I know I can do it.

Mr Simms: Thanks for the call, John. I'll see what I can do.

REFERENCES ON YOUR RESUME

There are two accepted ways of handling References on a resume, and your choice depends on your status as a job-seeker:

* If you are in the private sector, simply state "References Available Upon Request" and allow the employer the choice of asking you for references.

Or   * If you are seeking positions within government, social services, or education, include References by listing names, titles, addresses, and telephone numbers for each reference.

ILLUSTRATIONS AND EXAMPLES

The following illustrates various ways this component may be designed:

REFERENCES: Available Upon Request
_____

Or References Upon Request
_____

Or REFERENCES:

Dr. Samuel Davio
Professor of Education
San Diego State University
915 Pacer Street
San Diego, California 91765
Business Telephone: (415) 543-2211

Dr. Levena Smithson
Chairman, Department of Economics
State University
San Diego, California 91765
Business Telephone: (415) 543-9980

Mr. Albert Jackson
Executive Director
Association of Managers
905 Utica Street
Los Angeles, California 98765
Business Telephone: (415) 543-2211

Note that in this sample, *complete* addresses are provided, including zip codes and area codes. Note also that only the *business* telephone numbers of the references are listed.

PROBLEMS AND SOLUTIONS

How Many? *Question:* If I do list references, how many should I list?

Answer: This problem is common among resume writers. Again, as with all components discussed, the number of references greatly depends on the type of job you are seeking and the nature of the employer. The common practice is to list at least three references. Why? We aren't certain. Three is a nice number and represents a sample of people who know you and could provide a positive statement about you. Technical, educational, and other positions may require more—say five or seven references. However, don't overdo it.

How to Choose *Question:* That's fine, but which references should I choose? And what if I'm young and don't have previous employers?

Answer: Basically, you need to choose two persons who can affirm your professional and work related abilities and who can attest that you are a conscientious worker, hard-driving, and a good person to have "on the team." If you are just out of school and have not worked, then you need to select people who have observed you in work situations, whether mowing grass, working at church or at volunteer functions, or whatever! Finally, to round out your three references, select a person who can address your ability to relate to others and who can vouch for your integrity and worth. This person could be a clergyman, a co-worker, a friend of the family, an employer, or some other person who knows you well.

The Point Is: You need to select people who like you, who will say positive things about you, who feel that you can make a significant and meaningful contribution to *any* organization.

Caution: Remember, avoid selecting people who don't know you; it *has* happened—either the reference didn't know the applicant or else knew them so long ago that they had forgotten about the applicant and his/her job skills.

Contact Them *Question:* I'm still concerned about having to contact references—is it really necessary? After all, they will be contacted by just a few employers, and maybe no one will call them.

Answer: You're right, they will probably be contacted by very few people; but consider the following illustration:

Mary Sue was applying for a job. She listed as a reference a professor she had a year and a half before. The class was large and contact with the students was minimal. Mary Sue listed this person and did not contact him to indicate that he was a reference. The employer called and the professor, absent-minded anyway, denied ever knowing the person. It left a very poor impression and jeopardized the job opportunity. In fact, Mary Sue was not hired.

The Rule Is: If you list someone as a reference, contact that person and let him or her know! Here are additional reasons:

67 WITH FRIENDS LIKE YOU, WHO NEEDS ENEMIES?

* A brief and friendly chat with your reference updates your activities—you can indicate new growth areas and career directions.

   * You can describe the job opening and how your background and experiences fit.

      * You can bring out positives, reinforce information, and correct any misinformation or problems that might have existed previously.

         * If you send a copy of your resume to the reference, you will insure a positive image of yourself and provide a clear source of information about you when the employer calls.

            * If you send a thank you letter to your reference, you affirm a positive relationship with that person.

Maintain Contact It's a good idea to maintain contact with previous employers because you may need to get additional references, especially for higher paying jobs. Some organizations want names and telephone numbers of subordinates, peers, and superiors, for a total analysis of your personal and professional relationships.

You are now ready for Resume Action Step #8.

RESUME ACTION STEP #8

Objective: To *write* Component #8, References for your resume

Materials: Pencil and paper
Previous directories and business cards

Action Step: On a separate sheet of paper, list References for all previous positions (ten years). Include their addresses, titles, and telephone numbers.

Also, list three character references.

Think of References for every category (you can pick and choose later).

Here is the format:

1. Name of organization
2. Supervisor's name, address, telephone number (include area code)
3. Co-worker's name, address, and telephone number (include area code)
4. Someone you supervised—that person's name, address and telephone number (include area code)

Additionally, list three character references:

1. Name, address and telephone number
2. Relationship to you

Now, following the guidelines of this Chapter, *Write* the Reference component for your resume.

For additional examples and illustrations of layout and design, refer to the Case Study Section in Chapter 10.

When you have completed this component, put your paper aside and move on to the next component, Chapter 9. You will have an opportunity to put it all together later.

9

Functional, Chronological, or Combination

Which One Is Right for You?

HAVE IT YOUR WAY—
ALL RESUMES DON'T HAVE TO LOOK
ALIKE

There are many different forms and types of resumes. Everyone has a solution, and someone may tell you the exact opposite of what someone else has said! However, there are three generally accepted types:

* Chronological
    * Functional
        * The Combination

An additional adaptation is the Letter/Resume, which is covered later on in this chapter.

Pointers: Here are some important points about resume format:

* The format of the resume should fit the *personality* of the person.
    * It should be tailored for the specific *organization* where it is being sent.
        * The resume format should be selected to be *adaptable,* allowing you to adjust the resume easily to fit a variety of job openings.
            * The active job seeker will probably *rewrite* his or her resume frequently during the job search campaign.
                * A person must be open to a format which will be comfortable for them, one that they will be able to *defend* during a job interview.
                    * The resume format should also take into account the package—*you*—that it is representing. For example, You may have certain experiences in your background which require a particular resume format, as in the case of a person who is middle-aged but has little work experience. This person may choose a Functional resume which highlights *Skills* rather than Work History!

Let's look at these formats one at a time.

THE CHRONOLOGICAL RESUME

Of all resume formats, the Chronological is the most popular and widely accepted. It is *adaptable,* allowing you to "plug in" component parts, created during The Resume Experience, in order to best represent your strengths and abilities. The resume which follows, for instance, includes a Summary Of Qualifications, a Work History, and a description of responsibilities for the various positions held.

The primary feature of the Chronological resume is the inclusion of a Work Experience component. Your work history should always be listed in chronological order, thus emphasizing the most recent and working back.

The Advantages

* You can utilize components of the Resume Experience.
  * You can highlight a strong steady work background.
    * It provides the employer complete information.
      * It is a format familiar to most employers.
        * It provides the employer with a guide for interviewing.
          * It allows for easy, logical resume preparation.
            * It helps you stress the organizations you have worked for.

Figure 9-1 shows an example of a resume written in the Chronological format. Be sure to check Chapter 10, "Case Studies," for additional examples.

THE FUNCTIONAL RESUME

For Whom? Although this resume is not the most widely used, it has its place. It works for:

* Persons experiencing a dramatic career change,
  * Persons with absolutely no work background,
    * Those with a disastrous job history.

These job-seekers will find the Functional format a possible solution to minimizing such potential barriers to employment.

As with the Chronological resume, you can pull components from The Resume Experience and organize them to highlight qualifications, skills, abilities, and accomplishments for the various functions you have performed in your work/life experience.

Little The primary feature of the Functional resume is that the *Experience?* Work Experience is *omitted* completely.

Skills and Abilities   *Question:* Does that mean that you want everything to do with the Work Experience left out?

Answer: Not exactly. Remember! The Functional resume is designed to sell you on the basis of your *skills and abilities,* while minimizing barriers. So, you leave out dates of employment and names of organizations but include skills and abilities drawn from your job descriptions as well as your overall experience.

The Advantages

* It demonstrates skills and abilities for those having limited work experience.
  * You can use components from The Resume Experience (except the Work Experience component).
    * It demonstrates professional growth, which is useful for those in a career change.
      * It lessens the impact of a poor job history.

Figure 9-2 shows an example of a resume written in the Functional format. Be sure to check Chapter 10, "Case Studies," for additional examples.

THE COMBINATION

What Is It?   *Question:* Hold on a minute! I've been with some good companies and would like them listed; but I've also got some serious gaps in employment. It doesn't look like any format would work for me. What is recommended?

Answer: The Combination Chronological/Functional resume can solve that problem. Basically, you will have a Functional resume which will include some specifics from the Work Experience component, such as the names of organizations and perhaps some dates. As with the other formats you pull these specifics from The Resume Experience.

Careful!   The key advantage is: you highlight the organizations and dates without visibly displaying the barriers to employment in your Work Experience section. As you will see in the following example, the Combination format flexibly solves these barrier problems. But this format has a drawback: As in the case of the Functional resume, it can create suspicion in the employer's mind about the lack of complete information.

Figure 9-3 demonstrates an example of a resume written in the combination format.

Figure 9-1. Chronological Resume

R E S U M E

J. Martin Fischer
10900 Oak Road
Kansas City, Kansas 67823
Home Telephone: (816) 669-9987
Business Telephone: (816) 899-0098

CAREER OBJECTIVE: To administer a medium-to-large continuing education program for an urban university and to
develop innovative learning systems for adult
learners.

SUMMARY OF   *Have successfully administered adult education
QUALIFICATIONS: courses resulting in a 40% increase in enroll-
                     ments

                    *Implemented coordinating procedures which in
                     creased the delivery of adult education pro-
                     grams to over 60% of the metropolitan area .

                    *Ability to work independently, take direction,
                     fit in and work well with people at all levels

                    *Excellent written communication skills

EXPERIENCE:
1970 to Present   ASSISTANT DIRECTOR
                    Center for Continuing Education, University
                    of Kansas at Kansas City

                    Administer a program for adults in the
                    metropolitan area which includes programming,
                    developing educational programs, budgeting,
                    promoting, and supervising the activities
                    of eight staff persons. Taught non-credit
                    courses for the business community.

1967 to 1970   PROGRAM SPECIALIST

                    Center for Continuing Education,
                    University of Kansas at Kansas City

                    Reported to the Dean of the Center and was
                    accountable for the promotion and develop-

Figure 9-1 (cont.)

RESUME
J. Martin Fischer
Page Two

ment of courses for the adult community. Created and implemented a career development program for adults. Served as a co-leader for a task oriented group at a variety of conferences and workshops.

1965 to 1967   GRADUATE STUDENT

University of Kansas

Taught graduate level courses and undergraduate experiences in educational philosophy, history, and administration

EDUCATION: Master in Education, 1967, University of Kansas, Lawrence, Kansas. Major: Educational Administration; Minor: Guidance and Counseling

Bachelor of Arts Degree, 1965, Kansas State University, Mankato, Kansas. Major: Geography; Minor: Business Administration

Seminar: "MBO Goes to College", May, 1977, University of Colorado, Center For Managment and Technical Programs, Boulder, Colorado

RELATED
PROFESSIONAL
EXPERIENCE: Member, Adult Education Council, Kansas
      City, Kansas

Member, Phi Delta Kappa, Kansas City
      Chapter

PERSONAL: Birthdate: November 6, 1944

Marital Status: Married, two children

Health: Excellent

Interests: Tennis, Antiques, and
      Softball

REFERENCES: Available Upon Request

Figure 9-2. Functional Resume

R E S U M E

J. Martin Fishcer
10900 Oak Road
Kansas City, Kansas 67823
Home Telephone: (816) 660-9987
Business Telephone: (816) 899-0098

CAREER OBJECTIVE: To administer a medium-to-large education program for an urban university and to develop innovative learning systems for adult learners.

EXPERIENCE:

Programming - Programmed credit and non-credit courses for thirty locations within a large metropolitan area.

Development - Developed courses and other learning experiences to meet the unique needs of professional and social groups in and around a large metropolitan area.

Promotion - Developed promotional pieces for university sponsored programs to include layout and design, printing, and distribution. Developed television and radio commercials promoting continuing education services and activities.

Administration - Responsible for the coordination and personnel practices for a staff of eight persons. Supervised the activities of clerical help, student help, and professional programmers.

Innovation - Created and implemented a multimedia educational program for teaching adults career planning skills.

Teaching - Served as a graduate intern teaching education courses. Taught supervisory and managment courses for a noncredit supervisory development program.

Figure 9-2 (cont.)

RESUME
J. Martin Fischer
Page Two

<u>Human Relations</u> - Served as a group leader and facilitated task-oriented groups at seminars and conferences. Utilized human relations skills to solve personnel problems within organizations.

EDUCATION:

Master in Education, 1967, University of Kansas, Major: Educational Adminstration; Minor: Counseling and Guidance

Bachelor of Arts in Geography, 1965, Kansas State University, Major: Geography, Minor: Business Administration

RELATED
PROFESSIONAL
EXPERIENCE:

Member, Adult Education Council, Kansas City, Kansas

Member, Phi Delta Kappa, Kansas City Chapter

PERSONAL:

Birthdate: November 6, 1943 Health: Excellent

Marital Status: Married, two children

Interests: Tennis, Antiques, Softball

REFERENCES:

Dr. Seymour Miller
Dean, Center for Continuing Education
University of Kansas at Kansas City
1100 16th Street
Kansas City, Kansas 67845
Telephone: (816) 899-0089

Ms. Lynn Kigg
Program Director
Center for Continuing Education
University of Kansas at Kansas City
1100 16th Street
Kansas City, Kansas 67845
Telephone: (816) 899-0089

Mr. Clyde Riggs
Executive Director
Kansas Council on Business and Industry
Hallmark Center
Kansas City, Kansas 67864
Telephone: (816) 765-9876

Figure 9-3. Combination Resume

```
                        R E S U M E
                     J. Martin Fischer
                       10900 Oak Road
                  Kansas City, Kansas 67823
               Home Telephone: (816) 660-9987
             Business Telephone: (816) 899-0098
```

CAREER OBJECTIVE: To administer a medium-to-large education program for an urban univer-
sity and to develop innovative learning systems for adult learners

EXPERIENCE:

Programming - While with the University of Kansas, programmed credit
and non-credit courses for over thirty
locations within a large metropolitan
area resulting in a 40% increase in
enrollment.

Development - Developed courses and
other learning experiences to meet
the unique needs of professional and
social groups in and around a large
metropolitan area.

Promotion - Developed promotional
pieces for university-sponsored programs to include layout and design,
printing and distribution. Developed
television and radio commercials
promoting continuing education services and activities.

Administration - At the Center for
Continuing Education, Kansas City,
was responsible for the coordination
and personnel practices for a staff
of eight persons. Supervised the a
activities of clerical help, student
help and professional programmers.

Innovation - At General Dynamics
Corporation, created and implemented
a multi-media educational program
for teaching adults career planning
skills.

Figure 9-3 (cont.)

RESUME
J. Martin Fischer
Page Two

Teaching - Served as a graduate intern teaching educational courses.
Taught supervisory and management
courses for a noncredit supervisory
development program.

Human Relations - During 1974 to 1976,
served as a group leader and facilitated task-oriented groups at seminars
and conferences. Utilized human
relations to solve personnel problems
within organizations.

Contributing - Since 1967, have made
a solid and bottom line distribution
to such organizations as the University of Kansas, General Dynamics and
the Center for Continuing Education
at the University of Kansas.

EDUCATION: Master in Education, 1967, University
of Kansas, Major: Educational Administration; Minor: Counseling and
Guidance

Bachelor of Arts, 1965, Kansas State
University, Major: Geography, Minor:
Business Administration

RELATED
PROFESSIONAL
EXPERIENCES:
Member, Adult Education Council,
Kansas City, Kansas

Member, Phi Delta Kappa, Kansas City
Chapter

PERSONAL: Birthdate: November 6, 1943

Marital Status: Married, two
children

Health: Excellent

Interests: Tennis, Antiques, Softball

REFERENCES: Available upon request

THE LETTER/RESUME

A Mini-Resume   As a special adaptation of the various resume formats, the Letter/Resume has emerged as a significant alternative for the job seeker. It is increasingly considered to be a unique and creative way to represent yourself to a potential employer. The Letter/Resume is different from the cover letter because it is *more detailed* and includes *selected parts* of your resume in a paragraph format. In short, the Letter/Resume combines a cover letter with a resume and is sent instead of your regular resume. This does not mean that the Letter/Resume takes the place of a resume, but it is a creative format that can be a refreshing change. In addition, the

Important   Letter/Resume is particularly effective if you plan to make a follow-up call to the employer. But, don't allow the Letter/Resume to serve as a substitute for your resume! The Letter/Resume should be drafted from your resume when it has been completed. Be certain to present your resume during any job interviews.

The example in Figure 9-4 illustrates how J. Martin Fischer wrote his resume in a Letter format. It combines various information from all components of The Resume Experience and concludes with a statement requesting an interview.

It's Personal!   This chapter has demonstrated three types of resume formats plus one creative adaptation. No doubt there are several more; however, our purpose is to keep your resume simple, understandable, and dynamic. As you consider all types of formats for your resume, remember:

* If the shoe fits—wear it!

   * If you are comfortable with the format—choose it.

      * If it represents you in dynamic and positive ways—use it.

As we have said, you have to learn what your professional image is. Then you must learn your strengths and weaknesses and how to *best* represent them on a resume. Components can be interchanged, adaptations made, and creativity implemented. For example, if Education is a barrier to employment, then *minimize its impact* by placing this component towards the end of the resume.

Remember: Your goal is the creation of a powerful and dynamic resume that *gets jobs*.

To further assist you in deciding the format let's turn to Chapter 10 and see "What Others Have Done."

Figure 9-4. Letter/Resume

March 4, 1979

Dr. Anne Rogers
Dean, College of
  Continuing Education
State University
Whitefield, New Jersey

Dear Dr. Rogers,

Currently, I am with the University of Kansas at Kansas
City as an administrator of an adult education program.
It is our responsibility to meet the professional and
personal educational needs of the citizens of the city
of Kansas City.

In the past, I have personally been responsible for the
creation and implementation of several packaged educational programs for the professional community. These resulted
in a 40% increase in enrollments and increased visibility
for the university.

I understand that your university markets these types of
packages and has received several awards for their
uniqueness, applicability, and resourcefulness.

As a graduate of the University of Kansas, School of Education in Educational Administration in 1967, I was exposed
to this type of activity and, in fact, devised a multi-
media program for the training of adults in career planning.

I hold a Masters Degree in Education and am an active member of two educational associations.

I would appreciate the opportunity to meet with you to
discuss your programs and the possibility of associating
with your organization. I will be calling you within the
week to arrange an appointment.

Thank you, in advance, for your consideration.

Sincerely Yours,

J. Martin Fischer
Assistant Director

10
Case Studies
and Sample Resumes

Take a Look at
What Others Have Done

LEARNING FROM EXPERIENCE

Instead of including a random assortment of resumes without context or explanation, The Resume Experience now presents case studies of people facing real resume problems, and then recommends a specific approach tailored to the actual situation. Using this approach, you can see how the resume assists in solving a particular problem and is more meaningful as a result.

Since we see the resume as an experience in self-identification and growth it should be unique to a person's background.

We have found that many common problems, such as career changing, having too much education, not enough experience, a record of unemployment, being too young or too old, having held too many jobs, exist for *most* resume writers.

The Case Study approach allows you to *identify* with the person being described; then actually see how that person designed their resume to improve their career situation.

A word of caution: in the case studies you should not expect to find total answers to all career management problems but you should be able to identify with the various case studies and apply the principles to your unique situation.

GETTING THE MOST OUT OF CASE STUDIES

First, read the Case Study then review the sample resume by taking note of the way special problems were handled.

If the Case Study and resume are similar to your situation you might wish to create your resume in a similar fashion.

The Case Study section is purely fictitious and any resemblance to actual situations and persons is coincidental.

Each Case Study is presented in the following way: The Case Study is described. A Resume Design is then offered to highlight special considerations and problems confronting the person in question; certain strategies and techniques are mentioned.

The idea of this chapter is to gain a greater understanding of resumes and how to write them.

WOMAN/HIGH SCHOOL DIPLOMA/SOME EXPERIENCE/DESIRES BUSINESS

Case Study #1: Marsha L. Franklin

Marsha completed high school but chose not to continue with college. While in high school, she pursued a vocational education program which allowed her to work at a local real estate company on a work/study basis.

Her goal was to gain some work experience, earn a living, and eventually return to school. Her first position was as a secretary in a university setting. After a few years, she became a secretary/receptionist for a division of a national corporation at a higher salary.

From the receptionist position, Marsha was soon promoted to a secretarial position in the personnel office. Because of the growth of the company her duties began to include many administrative functions, such as interviewing, coordination, communications and decision making.

Marsha found these new challenges stimulating and wished to pursue a career in personnel. However, her career growth was blocked by the company because she didn't have a degree and they still considered her a secretary. As a result, Marsha decided to change companies.

Resume Design: Marsha selected a **Chronological** format which included a Summary of Qualifications in order to stress her abilities to work with people, be efficient, and communicate.

In the Work Experience component, Marsha felt that her experience and job title would be backed up by her boss, so she decided to take some liberties and list her title as Personnel Assistant instead of Secretary. Her job search is confidential so her current employer will not be notified.

Also, Marsha decided to relate her work experience in greater detail in order to minimize the impact of not having a degree. The Education component is listed on the second page.

Marsha typed her resume on an electric typewriter for a professional look and used an unusual type style to set her resume apart from others.

Also, Marsha purchased some good quality light blue paper and copied her resume on a dry copier machine using her own paper which made her resume look as if it were printed.

Here is Marsha's resume.

C O N F I D E N T I A L
R E S U M E

MARSHA L. FRANKLIN
23 SOUTH ELM STREET
NEW ORLEANS, LOUISIANA 70100
HOME TELEPHONE: (504) 711-3051
BUSINESS TELEPHONE: (504) 734-1122

CAREER OBJECTIVE: TO MANAGE THE PERSONNEL FUNCTION OF A SMALL TO MEDIUM-SIZE ORGANIZATION.

JOB GOAL: TO BE AN ASSISTANT PERSONNEL MANAGER WITH BROADER RESPONSIBILITIES TO ALLOW PROFESSIONAL GROWTH AND AN OPPORTUNITY TO CONTRIBUTE TO THE ORGANIZATION.

SUMMARY OF QUALIFICATIONS:

* ABILITY TO FIT IN AND WORK WELL WITH PEOPLE AT ALL LEVELS.

* COMPLETELY INVOLVED IN THE PERSONNEL FUNCTION INCLUDING INTERVIEWING, COORDINATION, EMPLOYEE RELATIONS, RECORD KEEPING, AND PERSONNEL CHANGES.

* HAVE DEMONSTRATED AN EXCELLENT ABILITY FOR ATTENTION TO DETAIL, ORGANIZATION, TIME PLANNING, AND PROBLEM SOLVING.

* PROVEN ABILITY TO DEAL WITH EMPLOYEES, THE PUBLIC, PROFESSIONAL ORGANIZATIONS AND CLIENTS.

* GOOD OVERALL COMMUNICATIONS SKILLS.

WORK EXPERIENCE:

AUGUST 1976 TO PRESENT: MARTIN MANUFACTURING, INC./HOUSTON, TEXAS.

AS PERSONNEL ASSISTANT, REPORTED DIRECTLY TO THE PERSONNEL MANAGER.

RESPONSIBILITIES FOR THIS MAJOR MANUFACTURER OF OIL FIELD EQUIPMENT INCLUDE RECRUITMENT ADVERTISING, COORDINATION OF INTERVIEWING SCHEDULES, INTERVIEWING, COORDINATION OF CORPORATE MOVES, PROCESSING OF NEW EMPLOYEES, ORIENTATION PRESENTATIONS TO MONTHLY TRAINING CLASSES, COORDINATION OF EMPLOYEE BENEFITS AND EMPLOYEE RELATIONS.

ACCOMPLISHMENTS INCLUDED ASSISTING IN THE SUCCESSFUL RECRUITMENT OF PERSONNEL FOR A NEW PRODUCT AREA AND A RESEARCH STUDY WITH CONCRETE RECOMMENDATIONS TO STREAMLINE COMMUNICATIONS AND ELIMINATE PROBLEMS.

MAY 1975 TO AUGUST 1976: SOUTHERN UNIVERSITY, DIVISION OF CONTINUING EDUCATION/NEW ORLEANS, LOUISIANA.

REPORTED DIRECTLY TO THE ASSISTANT DIRECTOR OF CONTINUING EDUCATION.

MARSHA L. FRANKLIN
CONFIDENTIAL RESUME
PAGE TWO

WORK EXPERIENCE (CONTINUED)

POSITION REQUIRED STRONG ABILITIES IN INTER-PERSONAL COMMUNICATIONS, TELEPHONE SKILLS, SECRETARIAL SKILLS, ORGANIZATIONAL AND TIME PLANNING SKILLS.

SEVERAL TIMES EACH YEAR, COORDINATED THE SCHEDULING OF MEETING PLACES AND LUNCHEONS FOR OVER 150 COURSES AND SEMINARS. ASSISTED IN REVISING THE SYSTEM FOR SCHEDULING SPACE FOR COURSES AND SEMINARS. INVOLVED IN THE DESIGN AND LAYOUT OF A MAJOR ADVERTISING SUPPLEMENT TO THE NEWSPAPER AND VARIOUS BROCHURES.

ASSISTED THE ASSISTANT DIRECTOR OF CONTINUING EDUCATION WITH HIS DUTIES AS PRESIDENT OF THE AMERICAN SOCIETY FOR TRAINING AND DEVELOPMENT. WAS AWARDED A CERTIFICATE OF COMMENDATION FROM A.S.T.D.

OCTOBER 1974 TO MAY 1975: JACKSON AND COMPANY REALTORS/NEW ORLEANS, LOUISIANA.

THIS SECRETARY/RECEPTIONIST POSITION INVOLVED A GREAT AMOUNT OF CLIENT CONTACT AND TELEPHONE POISE. SOME KNOWLEDGE OF REAL ESTATE FORMS AND PROCEDURES WAS REQUIRED. POSITION WAS PART-TIME.

EDUCATION: LAKE SENIOR HIGH SCHOOL, NEW ORLEANS, LOUISIANA, GRADUATED MAY 1975. GENERAL EDUCATION AND COLLEGE PREPARATORY COURSES. ACTIVE IN STUDENT AFFAIRS.

CAREER VOCATIONAL/TECHNICAL CENTER, NEW ORLEANS, LOUISIANA, ADMINISTRATIVE/SECRETARIAL COURSES.

PERSONAL: BIRTHDATE: FEBRUARY 11, 1957
HEALTH: EXCELLENT
MARITAL STATUS: SINGLE

INTERESTS: READING, TENNIS, VOLUNTEER ACTIVITIES

REFERENCES: AVAILABLE UPON REQUEST.

MAN/STUDENT/JUST GRADUATING/NO EXPERIENCE/DESIRES BUSINESS

Case Study #2: Douglas L. Marten

Doug was typical of many young students graduating from college. He had very limited work experience but had received a sound education with a B.A. degree in communications. He had planned to enter a career of Broadcast Journalism; however, most of the available positions required at least two or three years of experience for an entry level position.

Doug was a joiner during his high school and college years. He had participated heavily in intramural sports, fraternities, inter-collegiate clubs and organizations related to the communications field. He was bright and his transcript showed excellent grades.

Doug held various positions of leadership in clubs and other activities. He was a participant in organizing several events and activities and coordinated one of the best intramural programs in the city.

Resume Design: The employment barrier facing Doug in designing his resume is typical for most students graduating from high school or college—*no experience* in the world of work! Doug had never worked for an organization as a *salaried* employee, but he did possess certain skill areas that were applicable to a career in communications.

He selected a **functional** format for his resume. The reason is that it does not include a Work History section but stresses skill areas which illustrate responsibility, follow-up and (most importantly) maturity.

To further enhance his competencies in communications, Doug listed some activities and results of research projects and other course requirements as a communications major. For instance, he designed an educational program for children that would teach the differences between "right hand" and "left hand." This activity contributed to his understanding of "real life" communication problems and adds credibility to his resume.

Students often discount part-time positions, research projects, or other activities that bring them in contact with business and industry. These experiences help develop skills and understanding of the world of work!

Doug's resume appears on the following page.

```
                        R E S U M E
                     Douglas L. Marten
                     2621 M. Street N.W.
                   Washington, D.C.  20021
                 Home Telephone:  (202) 675-9876
                 Answering Service:  (202) 678-8741



CAREER OBJECTIVE:    To design and implement programs in broadcast
                     journalism and to use my skills in communications
                     to creatively develop innovative television and
                     radio dialogue.

EXPERIENCE:          Broadcast Journalism - Designed and developed an
                        educational program for children.  Received
                        recognition for its uniqueness and simplicity.

                     Communications - Edited and directed the develop-
                        ment of a newsletter to promote a major
                        intramural program for a large university.

                     Leadership - Coordinated a fund-raising drive
                        for a large volunteer organization that resulted
                        in a 60% increase over the previous year.

                     Research - Conducted a survey for a large
                        organization that measured the value of various
                        communication systems.  Resulted in the
                        implementation of a cost-reduction program.

EDUCATION:           Bachelor of Arts Degree, 1978, Georgetown
                        University, Washington, D.C.  Major: Broad-
                        cast Journalism; Minor: Communications.

RELATED              Member, Associated Students, Georgetown Univer-
PROFESSIONAL            sity, 1976-78.
EXPERIENCE:          Member, Alpha Chi Fraternity, 1973 - present.
                     Chairman, United Way Student Fund, 1977-78

PERSONAL             Birthdate:  June 3, 1956
INFORMATION:
                     Marital Status:  Single

                     Health:  Excellent

                     Interests: Rugby, tennis, outdoors

REFERENCES:          Available upon request.
```

MAN/STUDENT/SOME WORK EXPERIENCE/LACK OF DIRECTION/ DESIRES GOVERNMENT

Case Study #3: David Clemine

David's background indicated a history of part time jobs, periods when he was a school drop out, a stint in the military, a sour marriage, and finally returning to school at the age of 28.

David's barrier to employment was a lack of motivation and the fact that he was lacking direction in both his career and his life. He had changed majors about twelve times during his first experience with college. After his military years, he held a job related to his military occupational specialty—construction drafting.

David was talented: He possessed many skills he was unaware of; plus he was a skilled artist. Despite his investigations into various career fields and a sequence of visits to college counseling centers for interest inventories and other self-assessment programs he remained uncertain about his career direction. Then he learned about the field of appraising.

As an outdoor person Dave was a keen observer and analyst. He learned about appraisal work from a friend and began to research the field. Upon discovering that a degree was required he returned to school to major in business with an emphasis on Agribusiness. In addition, he attended basic courses offered by a professional association in the area of Rural and Ranch Appraising. He desired to be an appraiser for a government agency.

Resume Design: Basically, Dave needed a **Functional** resume, but needed to show some work experience in the way of organizations, dates, and locations. So he selected the basic format of a Combination resume.

In the functional area he needed to demonstrate skills in mathematics, economic analysis, observation, research, business, and related social, political, and agricultural subjects.

Attending appraisal schools plus designing educational experiences as part of his degree program demonstrated his sincere and conscientious desire to excel in his career field.

In addition, Dave spent three months volunteering to assist an appraiser in his work. This accomplished two things for Dave: First, it provided an actual appraisal experience; secondly, it gave him a reference from an experienced appraiser who could attest to his knowledge and skill.

He selected the Professional Profile heading to portray a professional image rather than one of a beginning job-seeker.

Also, Dave got the assistance of a printer to design, type-set and print the resume.

Dave's resume appears on the following page.

Work History

1977 to Present	Volunteer Appraiser Assistant, Leasehold Inc., Boise, Idaho.
1976 to 1977	Construction Draftsman, Hoop Associates, Spokane, Washington
1972 to 1976	Military service. Construction Draftsman, Fort Belvoir, Virginia
1969 to 1972	Part time positions including waiter, ski instructor, and volunteer fire fighter
1968 to 1969	Student, University of Washington

Education

Bachelor of Science in Business Administration. In Progress, Boise State University, Boise, Idaho. Major: Agribusiness; Minor: Accounting

Ranch Appraisal School, June 5-10, 1977. American Society of Farm Managers and Rural Appraisers, Boise, Idaho

Seminar: "The Professional Appraiser," September 9-10, 1978, American Society of Farm Managers and Rural Appraisers, Spokane, Washington

Diploma, West High School, Spokane, Washington, 1968

Personal Information

Birthdate: July 15, 1950
Health: Excellent
Interests: Outdoor activities, Sports

References:

Mr. Richard Dunn, A.R.A.
912 5th Street, Suite 610
Boise, Idaho 83700
Business Telephone: (208) 674-0987

Mr. Nick James
Executive Director
Society of Appraisers
1100 16th Street
Washington, D.C. 20202
Business Telephone: (202) 998-8976

Mr. Carl Nywot
Hoop Associates
800 10th Avenue
Spokane, Washington 99220
Business Telephone: (509) 324-3321

PROFESSIONAL PROFILE

David Clemine

7161 North Pike Circle
Boise, Idaho, 83700
Home Telephone: (208) 421-6723
Business Telephone: (208) 674-0987

Career Objective:

To appraise land for purposes of sale or lease for a governmental agency.

Experience:

Appraising—Have appraised eight properties via the income approach and assisted in the appraising of an additional seven properties using the market data approach.

Mathematics—Investigated mathematical solutions to construction designs and devised formulas for indexing concrete and steel structures.

Accounting—Skilled in completing cost-benefit analysis on income and commercial property while an appraisal assistant.

Economics—As part of a research project, developed charts to better analyze the environmental and economic impact of strip mining in rural areas.

Design—Skilled in layout and design of illustrations, charts, graphs, maps and have published several graphics in major military and educational sources.

Coordination—Coordinated the activities and events of a community career education fair during 1976-77.

Social Sciences—Proficient in understanding and applying social and political concepts to complex urban and regional planning problems.

Received recognition for devising a system to divert water in order to protect the development of a multi-purpose recreational area.

WOMAN/DIVORCED/RETURNING TO SCHOOL/DESIRES BUSINESS

Case Study #4: Marlene J. Haskins

Marlene received her degree in literature with a minor in history. While in college, she obtained some work experience in fast foods, customer service and bookkeeping. Marlene also got married during her school years, becoming a housewife after graduation.

After eleven years of marriage and three children, Marlene divorced her husband and was forced to return to full-time employment. Her only work experience in a skilled area was in bookkeeping.

Marlene wants to pursue a job in bookkeeping with the goal of becoming an accountant. Additionally, she intends to supplement that experience with courses in accounting and has enrolled at the local university.

Resume Design: Marlene's strategy involved listing a Summary of Qualifications to bring out specific communications and bookkeeping skills which she possessed. She selected a **combination** format for her resume.

Education is her main strength so she decided to list it next. She also included a summary of her current educational experience which tied into her career goal.

In the Work Experience component she chose to relate her full-time experience in a single listing. If she listed each employment date chronologically from her first full-time job to the present, it would have been obvious that her last full-time employment ended in 1969. She had since been involved in various volunteer activities and had significant responsibilities as a housewife and considered these to be bona fide work experiences.

To avoid a potential barrier to employment, Marlene listed her marital status as "single" in the Personal Component. She felt that if she left it out the employer might make assumptions. Also, she didn't want the fact that she had "kid responsibilities" and that she was divorced to keep her from getting interviews.

Marlene selected a very attractive light grey paper for her stationery and also purchased additional sheets to copy her resume on with a dry paper copier. This approach gave her resume and correspondence a coordinated look.

Marlene's resume is on the next page.

R E S U M E

MARLENE J. HASKINS
29 So. Oak Street
Lake Oswego, Oregon 97034
Residence: (503) 635-2108

CAREER GOAL: To gain a broad base of knowledge in accounting and finance with the objective of becoming a CPA.

SUMMARY OF QUALIFICATIONS:

* Have successfully supervised and trained book-keeping personnel.

* Consistently met deadlines on accounting clean-up and reconstruction projects as well as monthly payrolls, tax assignments, and financial reports.

* Have demonstrated excellent attention to detail, organization, and time management.

* Ability to work independently, take direction and fit in and work well with people at all levels.

EDUCATION: Currently attending the University of Oregon to study accounting with the objective of entering the Graduate School of Business. Have successfully completed 9 hours with a 3.5 G.P.A.

University of Southern California, Los Angeles, California, completed a Bachelor of Arts degree in Literature and a minor in History, graduated 1968, earned 85% of expenses.

WORK EXPERIENCE:

1964 to present: Volunteer Activities

Experience and skills included organization, budgeting, planning and coordination or various projects. Worked with numerous professional people. Successfully organized a 50-person volunteer effort which raised $300,000 for a hospital expansion.

MARLENE J. HASKINS
Resume
Page Two

WORK EXPERIENCE
(CONTINUED)

Full-Charge Bookkeeper

Responsibilities included various accounting and analysis functions, including monthly write-up; financial reports; payroll reconciliations and quarterly reports; and year-end analysis, scheduling and tax returns. Experience in cash flow analysis, breakeven charts, cash to accrual conversions, statements of change in financial position and various clean-up and reconstruction projects.

Supervised and trained personnel. Instigated and implemented new and better systems for accounts as needed.

Fast Food Franchise Manager

Managed the afternoon and evening operation of a fast food franchise. Supervised eight employees including training, scheduling, and evaluations. Was accountable for inventory control, cash, and closing.

PROFESSIONAL ORGANIZATIONS: Member, League of Women Voters and United Way

PERSONAL: Birthdate: April 26,1946
Marital Status: Single
Health: Excellent

REFERENCES: Available upon request.

MAN/MILITARY/RETURNING TO SCHOOL/ DESIRES EDUCATION

Case Study #5: Donald T. Smith

Donald entered the military service immediately following graduation from a polytechnical institute. Because of some excellent duty assignments, Donald was promoted quickly and gained considerable technical experience which focused on military technology, engineering, and weapons research. He had a top secret clearance and was cited frequently for his contributions to research and development of military equipment. In short, he had a very distinguished military career.

Prior to his retirement from the military, Donald decided to pursue graduate work in higher education administration and student personnel services. Since this represented a radical departure from military technology, the preparation of Don's resume required a lot of tact. He had to demonstrate administrative experience, skill in human relations, and an ability to formulate budgets.

Resume Design: To highlight education and training and minimize the technical aspects of his background, Don had to draw out experiences in which he was responsible for training. Consequently, he selected a **combination** resume with an experience paragraph. In the service Donald conducted several training programs and was able to demonstrate competence in organizing lesson plans and applying principles of learning. His last assignment with the military dealt with training and staff development. He did have administrative skills and was currently taking courses in learning theory, administration, and counseling as part of a graduate program.

Although Don had a very distinguished military career, he needed to create the impression that his military orientation was over and that he was now thinking and acting like an educational administrator. References to the military experience were minimized and he accordingly avoided the use of abbreviations and military phraseology in the resume.

Donald had received a job lead as an "evening administrator" for a local community junior college, and this became his job goal.

Donald's resume appears on the next page.

PROFESSIONAL PROFILE

DONALD T. SMITH
899 Huckleberry Road
Martinez, California 94553
Home Telephone: (415) 712-1116
Office Answering Service: (415) 986-9112

CAREER OBJECTIVE: To administer programs in higher education and to utilize my skills in human relations, teaching, and communications to improve the overall efficiency of an institution of higher learning.

JOB GOAL: To administer the after-hours program of a medium-sized community junior college and to teach in the areas of administration, educational psychology, and communications.

EXPERIENCE: Currently administering the training and staff development function of a military unit. Designed and implemented relations which resulted in an organization-wide acceptance of the program.

Skilled in budget analysis to include information, projection, cost-budget analysis, and implementation of cost savings programs.

Currently engaged in an educational program focusing on the practical application of administrtation theory and organizational behaviors.

Researched and designed a program to implement management by objectives program for colleges and universities and was instrumental in the design and implementation of a master plan for a large urban university.

Have demonstrated an excellent ability for organization, time management, and attention to detail.

A high achiever with a desire to effectively communicate with all levels of an organization and make significant contributions.

EDUCATION: Doctor in Education, anticipated graduation, 1980, University of San Francisco. Major Areas: Educational Administration; Educational Psychology; Research, Evaluation, and Measurement; and Business Administration.

Masters in Education, 1976, University of San Francisco. Major: Educational Administration.

DONALD T. SMITH
Professional Profile
Page Two

Seminar: "EEO and the College Administrator." April 1977, University of San Francisco, Center for Management Development, San Francisco, California.

Seminar: "Time Management," October 1976, American Management Association, San Francisco, California.

Bachelor of Science Degree, 1958, Chicago,Institute of Technology, Chicago, Illinois.

RELATED PROFESSIONAL EXPERIENCE:

Member, Doctoral Affairs Committee, University of San Francisco, School of Education, 1977 - present.

Member, Faculty Evaluation Committee, University of San Francisco, School of Education, 19/7- present.

Recognized for major contribution in the design of a Master Plan for the University of San Francisco, 1977.

PERSONAL:

Birthdate: January 13, 1936
Marital Status: Married, four children

Health: Excellent
Interests: Parachutist, outdoor enthusiast, automobile repairing, family.

REFERENCES:

Dr. Wallace Smith
Director, Higher Education Program Area
School of Education, University of San Francisco
San Francisco, California 94100
(415) 666-8800

Dr. Bernard Hughes, Professor, School of Education
University of San Francisco
San Francisco, California 94100
(415) 666-8800

Mr. Irving Snall, Director of Outreach Education
Northern California Community College
Martinez, California 94553
(415) 712-7112

WOMAN/NO DEGREE/RE-ENTERING JOB MARKET/SOME WORK EXPERIENCE/ DESIRES BUSINESS

Case Study #6: Florence B. Whitting

A common occurence in our modern society is the re-entry of women into the work force. This particular case is not representative of all women who desire a career change, but represents the most common as far as the creation of a dynamic resume. Professional career women usually can relate both experience and skill areas to new careers; however, women returning to the work force have a gap in their backgrounds that is difficult to reflect on the resume. They often feel out of touch with the world of work and are apprehensive to express their true and positive skill areas on a resume. Such is the case of Florence.

Upon graduating from high school, Florence became employed as a secretary in a pharmaceutical firm. She worked for about a year and a half, met her husband, married and spent the next twenty-five years of her life raising a family. She worked as a housewife and in volunteer activities eventually enrolling in a data processing certificate program at a local community junior college. She is currently a volunteer bookkeeper for her church and has taken considerable accounting course work in preparation for the data processing certificate.

Returning to school was intimidating enough to Florence to make her feel uncomfortable about writing a resume designed to "sell" her to the data processing field. Her first step was to become confident in the skill areas she possessed and become aware of the positive aspects of her self and her personality.

Florence was motivated to make a career change from being a housewife to becoming a systems analyst. She liked data processing and was one of those persons who enjoyed complexities and mathematical formulas. She was a keen observer and could make a fair and honest evaluation of situations. In short, she had the right ingredients to become a first class systems analyst.

Resume Design: The question is: "how does one become a systems analyst after twenty-five years as a mother and housewife?" The resume had to demonstrate that Florence would be an effective systems analyst. Fortunately, she could demonstrate skill areas in programming and key punch operation as a result of her experience in the community college program. Consequently, she selected a **functional** resume. When she completed the certificate she applied the credits toward a bachelors degree at a local university and began completing her degree in business.

Florence could also show other skill areas. She was organized, mature, level-headed and demonstrated good administration abilities as evidenced by her volunteer activities.

Florence's resume appears on the next page.

```
                        R E S U M E

                  FLORENCE B. WHITTING
                  6601 W. Ninth Avenue
                  Omaha, Nebraska  68100
               Home Telephone:  (402) 212-2981
```

CAREER OBJECTIVE: To analyze systems and procedures for a medium to large
                      organization and to use my skills in research, mathe-
                      matics, and accounting to improve the technical programming
                      of a business unit.

JOB GOAL: Seek a position as a computer programmer.

EXPERIENCE: <u>Programming</u> - Skilled in computer programming using
                         cobol and basic languages.
                      <u>Analysis</u> - Developed skill in analyzing flow charts,
                         programs, and systems procedures.
                      <u>Accounting</u> - Served as a bookkeeper for a large church
                         and was instrumental in implementing an accounting
                         procedure that improved the overall efficiency of
                         church operations.
                      <u>Mathematics</u> - Formulated mathematical designs for various
                         projects and problems and am competent in the mathe-
                         matical analysis of complex systems and procedures.
                      <u>Organization</u> - Highly organized with demonstrated leader-
                         ship skill in coordinating and motivating volunteer
                         workers.
                      <u>Human Relations</u> - Able to work well with people, accept
                         assignments, work independently, and make significant
                         contributions to an organization.

EDUCATION: Bachelor of Science in Business Administration (in progress),
                         University of Nebraska at Omaha, Major: Management
                         Technology; Minor: Accounting.

                      Certificate in Data Processing, 1978, Southwest Community
                         College, Omaha, Nebraska.

                      Diploma, 1952, West High School, Omaha, Nebraska.

RELATED PROFESSIONAL Member, Professional Women in Business, University of
EXPERIENCE: Nebraska at Omaha, Student Chapter, 1978 - present.

PERSONAL: Birthdate: October 4, 1934
                      Marital Status: Married, four children
                      Health: Excellent
                      Interests: Interior decorating, floral arranging, and
                         outdoor recreation.

REFERENCES: Available upon request.

WOMAN/DEGREE/RE-ENTERING THE JOB MARKET AFTER 20 YEARS/NO EXPERIENCE/

Case Study #7: Lois W. Wimmer

Lois, after 20 years of marriage and an almost grown family, was faced with a dilemma. Her husband's job was in jeopardy. His last two moves had been lateral and he was having serious doubts about his career direction as well as his life plan. At 43, he was right in the middle of a mid-life crisis. As a result, Lois was considering returning to work.

Lois had received her degree in education but chose to be married and raise a family. Her education was completely taken care of by her father so she had no need to work. Other than a sixty-day Christmas job in high school, she had no work experience.

Lois had been content being a housewife and raising her family. She had few outside interests and made no attempts to become involved in activities or pursue personal development. However, Lois had become quite skilled in handicrafts and had been making different items each year as Christmas gifts. She decided that her other major skill was raising and dealing with children as well as organizing a household.

Lois spent time thinking and asking people's opinions about what areas of work she should go into. Three areas kept coming up: manufacturing arts and crafts gifts, working in an arts and crafts retail store, or working in a children's day care center.

After careful consideration, Lois decided that it would be kind of fun to work in an arts and crafts store—even to become a store manager. She determined she wasn't ready for her own business and she was "burned-out" on supervising kids.

Resume Design: Lois had no alternative but to design a **functional** resume. She wanted to emphasize her creative talents, organizing abilities, attention to detail and her ability to work with people.

Here is Lois' resume.

```
                          R E S U M E


LOIS W. WIMMER
1411 So. Jay Street
Oakland, California  94600
(707) 893-2130


JOB OBJECTIVE:      To work as a retail salesperson and arts/
                    crafts consultant in an arts and crafts store.


SUMMARY OF
QUALIFICATIONS:     * Ten years experience creating and assembling
                      arts and crafts projects.

                    * Have demonstrated an excellent ability for
                      attention to detail as well as fast completion
                      time.

                    * Ability to design own projects.

                    * Good knowledge of all types of materials and
                      procedures.

                    * Willingness to work hard and make a positive
                      contribution.

                    * Have always gotten along well with people.

                    * Have been told by others that my personality,
                      problem-solving abilities, and caring nature
                      are all positives.

EDUCATION:          Bachelor of Arts Degree, graduated 1957, San
                       Jose State University, San Jose, California.
                       Major: Education; Minor: Art, Active in student
                       affairs and sorority leadership.


PERSONAL:           Birthdate:  February 21, 1936
                    Health:  Excellent
                    Marital Status:  Married


INTERESTS:          Arts and crafts, family outings, reading

REFERENCES:         Available upon request.
```

97

MAN/CAREER CHANGER/DESIRES BUSINESS

Case Study #8: Donald E. Sutherlund

Statistics indicate that some eight out of ten Americans are dissatisfied with their jobs. Don is one of the eight. He is an ex-minister, has had some industrial experience and currently is an administrator at a local college.

Personally, he comes across very effectively. He looks and dresses well, is tall, good-looking and has a strong powerful and commanding voice. He is sincere, conscientious, dedicated, loyal to an organization and is a good communicator. He has a lot of positive aspects but he is dissatisfied and desires a career change. His motives seem to lie with job satisfaction and a desire to make a higher salary. He is married with three children and is active in several community and professional associations.

He enjoys meeting and working with people and wants the freedom to keep his own time and set his own appointments.

Resume Design: The primary barrier confronting Don in his resume is a lack of experience in sales and his stint as a minister. To overcome this, Don needs to identify the skills required for a successful sales career and then demonstrate those same skills in the experience he already has! Since most of Don's background is in training and education he decided to enter the field as a sales trainer, allowing him to make the best possible use of his background.

To minimize the impact of his church-related experience, Don selected a **Combination** resume format: He combined a Summary of Qualifications paragraph with an "Experience" paragraph and indicated his work affiliations there. There is no Work History component and the resume emphasizes the positive contributions he could make to a sales and marketing organization.

As the resume indicates, the primary skill area involved is that of motivation and the ability to communicate. Risk-taking ability is also an important skill area, along with an understanding of adult education and the training process. These skills are stressed while education and work experience are minimized.

Instead of listing his doctorate or master's degree, he only listed his bachelors degree and a series of sales training seminars to stress his interest and enthusiasm for the sales field.

Further, he only lists organizations and professional societies which are related to the career objective. His educational and religious affiliations are minimized to increase the positive impact of his resume on the sales field.

Since he looks very young for his age and is entering the sales field late in life, it may be to his advantage to use a photograph.

Here's Don's resume.

CONFIDENTIAL PROFESSIONAL PROFILE

DONALD E. SUTHERLUND
4000 E. Oak Avenue, Apt. 910
Cleveland, Ohio 44100

Home Telephone: (216) 777-3612
Business Answering Service: (216) 674-1112

CAREER OBJECTIVE: To utilize my communication and human relation skills to
train personnel in motivation, sales, and marketing strategies.

SUMMARY OF   *As staff trainer, designed and implemented motivational training
QUALIFICATIONS: programs for a major west coast manufacturing firm.

*As a vice-president of a community college, developed and
initiated a community/public relations program that improved
the image of the college activity and resulted in an increase
in enrollments of 150%.

*Created and led workshops in human relations, planning, and
sales resulting in an organization-wide acceptance of the program
and improved organizational effectiveness.

*As staff member and leader of three churches, provided leader-
ship and motivation for fund raising and public relations
activity.

*Skilled at motivating people and gaining organizational and
program support.

EDUCATION: Seminar: "Professional Selling Skills," March 1977,
Xerox Corporation, Dayton, Ohio.

Seminar: "Telephone Techniques," July 1976, Sales Training
Institute, Cleveland, Ohio.

Seminar: "Communication & Persuasion," December 1978, Center
for Management Development, Daccron Industries, Cleveland, Ohio.

Bachelor of Arts Degree, 1956, Nebraska Wesleyan University,
Lincoln, Nebraska. Major: Theology, Minor: Psychology.

RELATED   Member, South Suburban Chapter of SWAP, Cleveland, Ohio.
PROFESSIONAL
EXPERIENCE: Member, Treasurer, 1977-78, American Management Association.

Member, Kiwanis International.

PERSONAL: Birthdate: May 2, 1933
Health: Excellent
Marital Status: Married, three children
Interests: Sports, people, tennis

REFERENCES: Available upon request

99

MAN/MILITARY/DESIRES BUSINESS

Case Study #9: Benjamin Sprockly

Persons retiring from military service present a special situation in the American labor market. They are highly skilled, young, and need to make a transition into civilian life that represents a radical departure from their military lifestyles.

The main objective of the transition is to match their skills to occupations in the civilian world. A second objective is to change their orientation from the military to the relatively unstructured lifestyles of civilian organizations.

A typical example is that of Benjamin J. Sprockly. Colonel Sprockly is retiring from the Air Force after 25 years of distinguished service. He has training in all aspects of the military; however, he specialized in materiel and contracts for the Air Force. Consequently, he can demonstrate considerable contact with business and industry and people in leadership and administrative positions.

At age 44, Ben needed to get a position with a growing industry, perferably one that required his skills in contracting and acquisition. He was seeking a small-to-medium organization with an informal operating procedure that offered a salary sufficient to support his lifestyle.

Ben is married with three grown sons.

Resume Design: A common characteristic of *most* military persons is that they overemphasize their experience and skill by using wordy paragraphs, military abbreviations, facts and figures. This style becomes a barrier to employment and can be a negative factor for some readers.

Ben selected a **chronological** resume with an Experience paragraph to highlight his skills. His accomplishments in the military are included in this paragraph and references to his military orientation are minimized through the use of short, concise, action-oriented statements.

Note that the resume avoids the use of military jargon and abbreviations and that the reference to the military is minimized. Again, the purpose is to focus on the outstanding skills Ben acquired while in the military and not the military organizations he commanded.

Ben's resume appears on the following page.

PROFESSIONAL PROFILE

BENJAMIN J. SPROCKLY
King Phillip Road
Burke, Virginia 22015

Home Telephone: (703) 932-4564
Business Answering Service: (703) 555-4446

CAREER OBJECTIVE: To administer a materiel and contracts division of a small to medium sized organization which would require a personal commitment for efficient and cost saving strategies.

EXPERIENCE: Planned, organized, budgeted, and directed a materiel and contracting program for a large governmental organization resulting in a cost savings of 50%.

Coordinated and implemented personnel policies resulting in improved communications and interpersonal relationships. Activity had a significant impact on the overall functioning and efficiency of the organization.

Analyzed, programmed, and implemented cost saving programs utilizing data collection and computer systems. Developed statistically oriented programs that resulted in improved efficiency and workforce reductions.

Designed, developed, and implemented bid packages to include source selections, change orders, contract awards, evaluations, and contracting procedures.

Skilled in human relations to include negotiations with domestic as well as foreign suppliers.

EDUCATION: Master of Science Degree, 1973, George Washington University, Washington, D.C. Major: Logistics Management.

Bachelor of Science Degree, 1956, Cornell University, Ithaca, New York. Major: Business Administration.

School, Professional Contracts Manager, United States Air Force, April - May, 1964.

School, Air Force Logistician, United States Air Force, November - January, 1962.

Seminar, "Purchasing Negotiations," 1977, American University, Washington, D.C.

WORK HISTORY:

1976 - Present	*Director, Contracts and Materiel Division, United States Air Force, Washington, D.C.
1973 - 1976	*Director, Materiel Section, Bolling Air Force Base, Washington, D.C.
1970 - 1973	*Program Manager, Materiel Section, Bolling Air Force Base, Washington, D.C.
1965 - 1970	*Contracting Officer, Supply Section, Andrews Air Force Base, Washington, D.C.
1952 - 1965	*Various positions of increasing responsibility in procurement, supply, management, and personnel administration.

RELATED PROFESSIONAL EXPERIENCE: Member, American Management Association
Co-author, "Materiel Management," Air Force News, January, 1976.

PERSONAL: Birthdate: November 7, 1934
Marital Status: Married; three sons
Health: Excellent
Interests: Aircraft, jogging, antiques

REFERENCES: Available upon request

WOMAN/CAREER CHANGER/DESIRES BUSINESS

Case Study #10: Kendra Baurer

At age 37, Kendra held a position as an administrative assistant for the chief executive officer at a large urban university. She was highly proficient in this position and was highly regarded for her ability to work with people and represent her employer at many functions where he was unable to attend.

Kendra, however, decided that she needed to change jobs to a position that would allow her more contact with people and less administration. She wanted to travel and work her own hours. Kendra was married but had no children. Her husband, Dave, was a high achiever and spent most of his time pursuing his career. Kendra felt hampered by her job—she saw no growth possibilities, and wanted a career in which she would feel more motivated and active.

Kendra analyzed her skills and then researched prospective careers before deciding to seek a sales position with a large computer firm.

Although she had some contacts within the firm, she needed to create a resume that would convince its sales executives of her ability to sell.

Resume Design: Kendra had no sales experience and no degree. What she did have was the ability to relate to and communicate with people. Using her contacts with the company, she identified those skills necessary for success in selling computers. Then she identified those skills that she already possessed which came closest to matching the ones determined to be necessary. She selected a **chronological** format for her resume.

In addition, she strengthened her position by joining sales-oriented organizations and enrolling in courses at a local Sales Training Institute.

Kendra wanted a bold, assertive looking resume. She chose a large type style, typed the resume on an office electric typewriter and then copied the resume on quality heavy paper using a dry copy machine. The paper was a very professional looking light grey which matched her stationery and envelope.

Here is Kendra's resume.

RESUME

KENDRA BAURER
1871 CHESIRE BRIDGE ROAD, N.E.
ATLANTA, GEORGIA 30300
HOME TELEPHONE: (404) 961-1117
BUSINESS TELEPHONE: (404) 658-8132

CAREER OBJECTIVE: To sell computer services and products and represent a large computer firm in the development of marketing strategies and procedures.

EXPERIENCE: Currently serving as an administrative assistant for the chancellor at a large urban university.

Successfully developed and implemented a public relation's program for the university and have met with a variety of professional and community groups as representative of the university.

Assisted in the design and development of promotional literature to sell the university's programs and services.

Instituted a booth for local educational fairs, responsibilities included design and development of the booth, displays, literature, faculty representations and promotions.

Skilled in the area of human relations and communications and am able to impress people through a positive, energetic approach.

Have demonstrated an excellent ability for attention to details, coordination, and time management.

WORK HISTORY:

MARCH 1978 to PRESENT: Administrative Assistant, Vice Chancellor for Administration; University of Toledo, Toledo, Ohio.

August 1974 to March 1976: Administrative Clerk, J. Weed and Sons, Toledo, Ohio.

December 1972 to August 1974: Receptionist, Brown, Bailey, and Buxton, Attorneys, Atlanta, Georgia.

October 1967 to December 1972: Secretary, Bowman Associates, Atlanta, Georgia.

KENDRA BAURER
RESUME
PAGE TWO

EDUCATION: Seminar, Telephone Techniques, Sales Training Institute, August, 1978.

Seminar, Sales Techniques, Sales Training Institute, April 1978.

Diploma, 1959, Jefferson Davis High School, Atlanta, Georgia.

RELATED PROFESSIONAL EXPERIENCE: Member, American Management Association, 1977-present.

Member, Dale Carnegie Institute, 1976.

PERSONAL: Birthdate: January 18, 1941
Marital Status: Married
Health: Excellent
Interests: Backpacking, jogging, tennis, golf

REFERENCES: Available upon request.

WOMAN/GAPS IN EMPLOYMENT/DESIRES CREATIVE FIELD

Case Study #11: Diana Berlingsonne

More and more people in our society have gaps in employment. Some of the reasons are legitimate, others are not. Almost all such gaps can be explained. Some explanations are more difficult than others. On a resume, however, gaps in employment almost always raise questions. This happens in the case of Diana.

Diana is a skilled person, but she didn't understand what her skills were. Currently, she is 34 years old and her background demonstrates an attempt at about every career field imaginable. She spent a great deal of time trying to "find herself" and her niche in society.

Diana was a social activist who traveled around the country participating in protests and the nouveau art movement. She established a pattern of working for awhile, becoming bored, quitting, travelling, running out of money, and then getting any kind of a job and starting the cycle once again.

At times during this period, Diana would return to school, work part-time and pay for an education. She earned a B.A. degree in Fine Arts after trying every major in the school catalog.

At age 34, she had several years of work experience, several credit hours of unrelated subjects, a degree, no career, little money, and a burning desire to settle into something stable.

Resume Design: Clearly, Diana had to minimize those frequent gaps in her employment record and demonstrate that she was now determined to settle into a career. In her resume there is no attempt to conceal her employment gap—partially because this would be impossible. Rather, they are explained in a way that represents Diana as a person undergoing reflection and reevaluation. Diana chose a **chronological** resume with a summary of qualifications.

As a creative person, Diana had the excuse of searching for the right career—one that would utilize her creativeness. Consequently, she used the words "leave of absence" to fill the gaps in her work history.

Her objective was to work in the field of commercial art. She enrolled in a School of Art to become skilled in the field and spent time developing influential contacts. She had won a lot of recognition and awards at art shows and now possessed an impressive portfolio for the beginning of her job search.

Diana wanted to demonstrate her creativeness by having her resume professionally type-set and printed. She did the design and layout herself.

Diana's resume appears on the following page.

Resume

Diana Berlingsonne

978 Rim Rock Road, Apt. T-2
San Diego, California 92100
Home Telephone: (714) 775-7754
Business Answering Service: (714) 911-8110

Career Objective

To utilize my artistic and design skills in the production and implementation of creative commercials and to develop unique mediums for advertising products and services.

Summary of Qualifications

• Currently assisting in the design, production, and implementation of advertising layouts for a major advertising agency.

• Coordinated and organized art projects for an urban university and assisted in the promotion of the school's art program.

• As a research assistant, analyzed and coordinated promotional campaigns for a variety of volunteer organizations in a major urban center.

• Creative talents include graphics, illustrations, set design and art production.

• Skilled in generating ideas and am known for creative, unique approaches to problem solving.

Education

Bachelor of Arts Degree, 1974, San Diego State University, San Diego, California. Major: Fine Arts; Minor: Communications

Diploma, 1962, Westwood High School, Ann Arbor, Michigan

Work History

1977 to present: Research Assistant, Macmer Advertising, San Diego, California

1976 to 1977: Leave of Absence

1975 to 1977: Administrative Assistant, Art Department, College of Liberal Arts, San Diego State University, San Diego, California

---

Diana Berlingsonne
Resume
Page Two

1974 to 1975: Leave of Absence for Travel Purposes

1973 to 1974: Receptionist, Harcourt and Smith, Attorneys, Carmel, California

1972 to 1974: Student Intern, San Diego State, San Diego, California. Traveled as part of a special program in cooperative education.

1970 to 1972: Waitress, Blue Spruce Inn, Lake Tahoe, California

1969 to 1970: Reseach Aid, City College of New York, New York City, New York

1967 to 1969: Student, University of Arizona, Phoenix, Arizona

Related Professional Experience

Student Member, Advisory Council, New School of Art, San Diego, California, 1977 to present

Affiliate Member, Metro Area Council on Commercial Art, San Diego, California

Personal

Birthdate: April 17, 1944
Marital Status: Single
Health: Excellent
Interests: Sketching, Backpacking, Sailing

References

Mr. Arthur Sontage
Director, Metro Area Council on Commercial Art
916 14th Avenue, Suite 911
San Diego, California 92100
(714) 111-1161

Ms. Shiela Dunham
Alco Art Products
#1 Tenle Circle
San Diego, California 92101
(714) 777-7771

Mr. Herion Quigg
Instructor, New School of Art
1601 New Rochester Road
San Diego, California 92105
(714) 611-1611

MAN/FREQUENT JOB CHANGES/DESIRES EDUCATION

Case Study #12: Robert L Simmons

With the advent of the art and science of job search and career management, plus the frequent news articles suggesting that people are unhappy with their jobs, there has been an increase in the frequency of job changes by the American worker.

Organizational loyalty, an integral part of the work ethic, has gone out of fashion to the point of seeming completely out of step with the times. Job changing has become more and more acceptable. Although there are still employers who consider people with a job-jumping history to be unstable and incapable of holding down secure positions. This too, is changing.

Robert Simmons is a job-jumper. He has been an educator, mainly in the area of administering educational programs to the adult community. It is very common in his profession to change positions frequently, often as much as once every two to three years. He lived in the East in a metropolitan area which had several institutions of higher learning which conducted similar programs. Bob and his peers all moved frequently and the practice was acceptable among adult educators.

Bob, however, wants to work for a large organization that makes a total commitment to training and development. He wants security and is willing to remain with the organization for many years if the job is rewarding. His primary barrier is "frequent job changes."

Bob holds a masters degree in educational administration and has attended several training related seminars.

Resume Design: To "sell" himself to the training and development profession, Bob needed to minimize the impact of his job changing. To do this, he stressed skill areas in the Experience paragraph along with accomplishments. At times, he held two or three positions with the same organization; so he combined those into one.

He also combined two short term jobs into one and listed himself as a "consultant." This was proper as long as he contacted the two organizations and explained his proposed job title on the resume.

Bob's **chronological** resume appears on the following page.

R E S U M E

ROBERT L. SIMMONS
1862 EAST BERRY WAY
ARVADA, COLORADO 80003

HOME TELEPHONE: (303) 423-0967
OFFICE TELEPHONE: (303) 689-8721

CAREER OBJECTIVE: TO ADMINISTER THE TRAINING PROGRAM FOR A LARGE INDUSTRIAL ORGANIZATION AND TO USE MY SKILLS IN COMMUNICATION, LEADERSHIP, AND ADULT LEARNING TO DESIGN AND IMPLEMENT EDUCATIONAL PROGRAMS.

EXPERIENCE: DESIGNED, DEVELOPED, AND IMPLEMENTED TRAINING PROGRAMS FOR BUSINESS AND INDUSTRY IN SALES TRAINING, SUPERVISORY TRAINING, CAREER DEVELOPMENT, AND EXECUTIVE DEVELOPMENT FOR A MAJOR URBAN UNIVERSITY.

DESIGNED AND IMPLEMENTED A LEADERSHIP PROGRAM THAT WAS EVENTUALLY USED TO TRAIN OVER 600 EXECUTIVES IN ORGANIZATIONS THROUGHOUT A MAJOR METROPOLITAN AREA.

TAUGHT, ADMINISTERED, AND PROGRAMMED CONTINUING EDUCATION COURSES, WHICH INCLUDED CREDIT COURSES, NON-CREDIT COURSES, WORKSHOPS, SEMINARS, AND CONFERENCES FOR BUSINESS, INDUSTRY, AND GOVERNMENT.

SKILLED IN THE AREA OF PUBLIC RELATIONS AND COMMUNICATIONS AND HAVE DEVELOPED POSITIVE WORKING RELATIONSHIPS WITH ALL TYPES OF ORGANIZATIONS.

WORK HISTORY:
PRESENT - CONSULTANT, METRO STATE UNIVERSITY AND STATE UNIVERSITY, WASHINGTON, D.C.

1976-77 COORDINATOR, CONTINUING EDUCATION PROGRAMS, GEORGE MASON COLLEGE, ANNANDALE, VIRGINIA

1975-77 ASSISTANT DIRECTOR, CONTINUING EDUCATION THE AMERICAN UNIVERSITY, WASHINGTON, D.C.

1974-77 PROGRAMMER, CENTER FOR CONTINUING EDUCATION, MARYLAND STATE UNIVERSITY, BOWIE, MARYLAND

1972-74 COORDINATOR, CIVIL DEFENSE EDUCATION PROGRAM, WASHINGTON, D.C.

1969-72 INSTRUCTOR, EMERGENCY PREPAREDNESS PROCEDURES, U.S. ARMY INTELLIGENCE SCHOOL, WASHINGTON, D.C.

1967-69 TEACHER, FAIRFAX COUNTY SCHOOLS, FAIRFAX, VIRGINIA

ROBERT L. SIMMONS
RESUME
PAGE TWO

WORK HISTORY (CONTINUED)
1965-67 STUDENT, UNIVERSITY OF MARYLAND, COLLEGE PARK MARYLAND

1961-65 STUDENT, FEDERAL CITY COLLEGE, WASHINGTON, D.C.

1958-60 MILITARY SERVICE, HONORABLE DISCHARGE.

EDUCATION:
MASTERS IN EDUCATION, 1967, UNIVERSITY OF MARYLAND, COLLEGE PARK, MARYLAND. MAJOR: EDUCATIONAL ADMINISTRATION; MINOR: ADULT EDUCATION.

BACHELOR OF ARTS, 1965, FEDERAL CITY COLLEGE, WASHINGTON, D.C. MAJOR: BUSINESS; MINOR: EDUCATION

"HOW TO TRAIN," AMERICAN SOCIETY FOR TRAINING AND DEVELOPMENT, WASHINGTON, D.C. CHAPTER, NOVEMBER, 1972.

"EFFECTIVE LEADERSHIP," AMERICAN MANAGEMENT ASSOCIATION, WASHINGTON, D.C., MARCH, 1975

RELATED PROFESSIONAL EXPERIENCE:
PAST PRESIDENT, AMERICAN SOCIETY FOR TRAINING AND DEVELOPMENT, WASHINGTON, D.C., CHAPTER, 1975-76.

MEMBER, AMERICAN MANAGEMENT ASSOCIATION, 1975-- PRESENT.

PERSONAL:
BIRTHDATE: APRIL 5, 1940
MARITAL STATUS: MARRIED, THREE CHILDREN
HEALTH: EXCELLENT
INTERESTS: COOKING, WRITING, BOATING, GOLF

REFERENCES:
AVAILABLE UPON REQUEST

MAN/YOUNG MANAGER/NO DEGREE/ DESIRES BUSINESS

Case Study #13: Raymond Juan Rodriguez

The potential barrier of "lack of education" for a member of a minority can be a serious problem to the young person desiring a career in business. However, with the advancements in affirmative action programs and equal employment opportunity, minorities in the United States are making significant gains in managerial and executive positions.

Raymond Rodriguez is a case in point. He graduated from high school and immediately enlisted in the Army. He did a three year tour, mustered out and went to work for a fast-food chain; first as a waiter, then as a supervisor. Raymond is very personable. He likes people, is friendly and comes across as dynamic, enthusiastic and energetic.

At the time he prepared his resume, he was working for the United States Postal Service. Since he was a "bundle of energy," he soon became disenchanted with the policies, procedures, and operations of the postal service. He continually identified new ways of doing things within the post office but was frustrated in his efforts to implement them. Clearly, he was an "idea person," with capabilities of making significant cost-saving suggestions—but within the wrong organization.

He needed a change to satisfy basic psychological needs but was uncertain as to exactly what his new career should be.

Consequently, he entered a career counseling program offered by a local university to assess his vocational skills and abilities and help him with his career planning.

Ray was married and had one child. His home life was not the greatest, largely because of his frustrations regarding career decisions.

Because of the workshop, Ray was able to focus on the training and development profession. Because of his "people skills" and presentation skills, he could enter the field in several industries without a degree.

Resume Design: Ray selected to include a job goal to indicate that he is seeking an entry level position with a desire to eventually become a training manager. This strategy served to demonstrate a career plan of action plus the desire to develop himself as a professional trainer.

To reduce the impact of not having a degree, Ray enrolled in a university program as a business major. He also selected to use a "Professional Profile" heading to emphasize his concept of being a professional manager seeking opportunities in the training field.

In his resume, his life plan and qualifications are given first, while his work history and educational components do not appear until the second page. He needed to show the reader that he did possess professional training skills and that he was eager to learn and develop within his chosen career field. His "Summary of Qualifications" section highlights Special Skill areas that Ray possesses that are important for the training profession. Now take a look at Ray's **chronological** resume.

PROFESSIONAL PROFILE

RAYMOND JUAN RODRIGUEZ
6921 E. ROLAND STREET
LITTLETON, COLORADO 80211

HOME TELEPHONE: (303) 711-7112
BUSINESS TELEPHONE: (303) 750-1119

CAREER OBJECTIVE: To MANAGE THE TRAINING FUNCTION OF A MEDIUM TO LARGE ORGANIZATION.

JOB GOAL: To BE A TRAINING ASSISTANT FOR FIRST NATIONAL BANK OF DENVER.

SUMMARY OF QUALIFICATIONS:

* AS SUPERVISOR AND NIGHT MANAGER, EFFECTIVELY HIRED, TRAINED, AND EVALUATED THE WORK ACTIVITIES OF NUMEROUS PERSONNEL.

* EFFECTIVELY COORDINATED WITH DEPARTMENT HEADS AND MANAGERS TO PROCESS AND DISTRIBUTE MAIL.

* SKILLED IN WORKING WITH GROUPS OF PEOPLE AND AM AN EFFECTIVE PRESENTER TO LARGE GROUPS OF PEOPLE.

* ABILITY TO WORK INDEPENDENTLY, TAKE DIRECTION, FIT IN, AND WORK WELL WITH PEOPLE AT ALL LEVELS.

* DIRECTLY INVOLVED IN THE SUPERVISION OF THE WORK ACTIVITIES OF OTHERS.

* HAVE DEMONSTRATED ABILITY FOR ORGANIZATION, ATTENTION TO DETAIL AND TIME MANAGEMENT.

* PROFICIENT IN HUMAN RELATIONSHIPS

* PROFICIENT IN HUMAN RELATION SKILLS, AM A SELF-STARTER, TASK-ORIENTED INDIVIDUAL MOTIVATED TO BE PRODUCTIVE AND A MAJOR CONTRIBUTOR.

WORK HISTORY:

MAY 1973 TO PRESENT:
POSTAL SUPERVISOR, UNITED STATES POST OFFICE, LITTLETON, COLORADO

SEPTEMBER 1971 TO PRESENT:
STUDENT, UNIVERSITY OF COLORADO AT DENVER.

WORK HISTORY
(CONTINUED)

JULY 1972 TO OCTOBER 1973:
NIGHT MANAGER, GUFFIES HAMBURGERS, INC., LITTLETON, COLORADO.

TRAINED AND SUPERVISED 8 EMPLOYEES PLUS ACCOUNTABLE FOR OVERALL ACCOUNTING OF RECEIPTS.

AUGUST 1970 TO JUNE 1972:
NIGHT MANAGER, WORLD OF TACOS, INC., LITTLETON, COLORADO.

RESPONSIBILITIES INCLUDED GENERAL MANAGEMENT, SUPERVISOR, WASH CONTROL, TRAINING, AND SECURITY.

JULY 1967 TO JULY 1970.
MILITARY SERVICE, HONORABLE DISCHARGE.

EDUCATION:
BACHELOR OF SCIENCE IN BUSINESS ADMINISTRATION, ANTICIPATED GRADUATION, MAY 1979, UNIVERSITY OF COLORADO AT DENVER; MAJOR: PERSONNEL ADMINISTRATION, MINOR: PSYCHOLOGY (CURRENTLY IN TOP 20% OF CLASS).

DIPLOMA, LITTLETON HIGHSCHOOL, 1967, LITTLETON, COLORADO.

RELATED PROFESSIONAL EXPERIENCE:
MEMBER, ROCKY MOUNTAIN CHAPTER, AMERICAN SOCIETY FOR TRAINING AND DEVELOPMENT, 1977 TO PRESENT.

PERSONAL:
BIRTHDATE: JUNE 6, 1949
MARITAL STATUS: MARRIED, ONE CHILD
HEALTH: EXCELLENT
INTERESTS: PEOPLE, PLACES, SOFTBALL, SPORTS

REFERENCES:
AVAILABLE UPON REQUEST.

WOMAN/HANDICAPPED/DESIRES EDUCATION

Case Study #14: CeCelia Andrews

Despite our efforts to bring handicapped persons into the main-stream of life, handicaps represent a major barrier to employment. As with any other barrier, the goal of the handicapped person is to reduce the impact of the handicap and focus on those areas where the person can make a significant contribution to the organization.

CeCelia has a handicap. She was a victim of muscular disorder and has a speech impediment plus loss of the normal functioning of her right arm. Although considered healthy, CeCelia lived with her handicaps and experienced considerable discrimination during job interviews.

CeCelia was an educator. She had attended college and received a B.S. degree in secondary education with a major in social studies.

Her interests, however, centered in the area of sociology, particularly working with handicapped senior citizens. Her skill areas focused on leadership, communication, fund raising, and presentations. She was a competent and reliable individual who did not allow her handicaps to hold her down.

Resume Design: In CeCelia's case, there was little need to indicate "poor health" under the Personal component. Nor was there any need to indicate her handicap anywhere on the resume. Her handicap wasn't readily identifiable or hindering her normal functioning, so she actually had nothing to conceal. So, she chose to leave out the Health section.

A severe handicap should be stated in positive terms in the Health section of the Personal component. Since the objective of the resume is to stress positive skill areas, the person should complement his or her strengths by demonstrating a positive outlook on the handicap.

```
Health: Excellent, have successfully integrated a
        physical disability with my professional
        life.
```

On the next page is CeCelia's approach to a **chronological** resume.

R E S U M E

CECELIA RUTH ANDREWS
916 South Pierce
South Bend, Indiana
91260
Home Telephone: (914) 876-9834
Office Telephone: (914) 457-0900

CAREER OBJECTIVE: To administer a counseling program for handi-
                   capped senior citizens and to utilize my
                   communication and fund-raising skills in
                   designing and implementing self-help programs.

JOB GOAL: Program Director, Center for Gerontology Research

EXPERIENCE: Currently a staff member with a federally funded
                   community action center.

                   Designed and implemented an internal communica-
                   tion system that increased client visitations
                   by 20%.

                   Developed an evaluation of client services that
                   was used for the basis of obtaining federal funds
                   for gerontology services.

                   Created and implemented a public relations program
                   that resulted in improved community relations.

                   Used leadership and coordinating skills to raise
                   funds for the building of a community action center
                   for the elderly.

EDUCATION: Bachelor of Science Degree, 1973, University of
                   Notre Dame. Major: Secondary Education

                   "Grant Writing," U.S. Department of Health,
                   Education, and Welfare, November 1977.

                   "Administering the Volunteer Organization,"
                   Indiana University, March, 1978.

JOB HISTORY: November, 1976 - Present: Program Director, South
                   Side Community Action Center, South Bend,
                   Indiana.

                   August, 1973 - November, 1976: Faculty member,
                   Cook County School District #4, South Bend,
                   Indiana.

                   September, 1969 - June 1973: Student, University
                   of Notre Dame, South Bend, Indiana.

RELATED
PROFESSIONAL
EXPERIENCE: Secretary, Indiana Mental Health Association

                   Presenter, "Mental Health for Senior Citizens,"
                   South Bend Chapter, American Mental Health
                   Association, June, 1977.

                   Member, American Mental Health Association

PERSONAL: Birthdate: March 8, 1951

                   Marital Status: Single

                   Interests: Theater, tennis, backpacking, and
                   reading

REFERENCES: Available upon request.

MAN/EX-CON/DESIRES SOCIAL SERVICES

Case Study #15: Merle Jammerson

At age 43, Merle could be classified as a job-jumper. You name it and Merle has done it. He was a mechanic, a caddy, a dish washer, construction worker, railroad yard supervisor, and during his military duty, a cook.

Merle had one serious barrier to employment—he was an ex-con. He served time for a minor theft charge several years ago.

Since his release, Merle has been "into" humanitarianism. He was always known for his concern about the little guy or the disadvantaged. It was this attitude which encouraged him to seek a career as a probationary counselor.

Merle received help from the state employment service. He had no degree but had acquired a GED high school equivalency while in the military. He had his veteran's benefits and chose to return to school at age 40 to pursue a B.S. degree in education with a focus on rehabilitation counseling.

As he was approaching graduation, he needed to prepare a resume and begin job hunting.

Resume Design: The social services fields typically seek stable, dependable persons who will be reliable and provide ethical guidance services for their clientele.

Merle had to create his resume to stress the impact he has had on the lives of others and minimize his frequent job changes and his brief scrape with the law.

Further, the resume had to demonstrate that Merle was different now, that he was seeking a professional career and wanted to make a professional contribution. As the resume indicates, Merle had skills in human relations and experience in working with clientele served by probationary counselors.

In the resume, he demonstrates the *results* of his influence and interactions with these people. As indicated, Merle gets results and has an impact on the lives of people—a characteristic which is important for social services organizations.

He selected a **functional** format to downplay his work history and to stress his skills.

Merle's resume appears on the next page.

PROFESSIONAL PROFILE

MERLE JAMERSON
960 West 61st Avenue
Buffalo, New York 14200

Home Telephone: (716) 452-9601
Business Telephone: (716) 916-1117

CAREER OBJECTIVE: To counsel persons experiencing conflict in adjusting to probation and to design and implement career development programs to assist them in refocusing their lives.

EXPERIENCE:
Counseling: Extensive experience in design and implementing probationary charts; one-to-one counseling of ex-offenders in many areas; including career development and alcohol and drug abuse.
Human Relations: Successful in working with different groups and individuals on the design of community development programs.
Facilitation: Work effectively with all groups and am skilled in keeping a group task-oriented and producing results.
Supervision: Supervised the work of others and am effective in getting work accomplished via objectives and effective time management.
Job Development: In consultation with other public agencies, am skillful in identifying and developing new and potential jobs.
Crisis Intervention: Have successfully provided assistance in a variety of crisis situations resulting in the attainment of personal goals for clients.
Program Development: Designed and successfully implemented a career development program for probationary clients. The program showed a 60% increase in participation and 45% increase in job placements.

EDUCATION:
Bachelor of Science Degree (In Progress), State University of New York, Buffalo, New York, Major: Rehabilitation Counseling.

Diploma, General Education Development, 1958.

Workshop: "Counseling for Crisis," 1977, West Side Action Center, Buffalo, New York.

EDUCATION
(Continued)
Seminar: "Family Counseling," 1976, State University of New York, Counseling Department, Buffalo, New York.

Seminar: "Coping with the Judicial System," April 9-10, 1976, Syracuse University, Syracuse, New York.

RELATED PROFESSIONAL EXPERIENCE:
Member, New York State Personnel and Guidance Association, 1975 – present.

Member, Agency Counselor Division, New York, Personnel and Guidance Association, 1977 – present.

PERSONAL INFORMATION:
Birthdate: March 3, 1935

Interests: Helping others, volunteer work, natural history.

REFERENCES:
Dr. Daniel Gomez
Director Rehabilitation Program
State University of New York
Buffalo, New York 14200
(716) 629-7771

Ms. Cecelia Jones
Counselor
Youth Opportunity Program
1219 State Street
Buffalo, New York 14201
(716) 916-1461

Mr. Darrell Sandman
Program Coordinator
State Department of Social Services
Buffalo, New York 14202
(716) 831-6611

MAN/FORCED RETIREMENT/DESIRES BUSINESS

Case Study #16: Benjamin Whitfielder

Forced retirement presents a difficult situation for many people to face. Through no fault of their own, they suddenly find themselves without a job, but with several years of productivity ahead of them and the potential barrier of being "too old" for entry-level positions.

Such is the situation of Benjamin Whitfielder. Ben was 54 years old when the company to which he had devoted 19 years of his life drummed up a false theft charge against him in the hope that he would resign, saving them from having to pay his retirement. Ben did resign rather than confront them on the charge, but was now left with the problem of what to do with the rest of his active work life.

Ben's strengths were in managing, training, organizing, budgeting, merchandising, and general supervision. He was considered a "good man"—loyal to the organization and had good human relations skills. He still had family living at home and two of his children were in college. Ben had to find an occupation that would pay at least the salary he was making previously. His personality was passive, but he held strong convictions and had a good general appearance.

Having felt that he would stay with this company until retirement, Ben did little to create other options and opportunities. After his termination, Ben researched other areas and settled on property management as his area of interest.

Resume Design: Since Ben's strengths were in administering and directing people, property management seemed a viable alternative. His resume, then, had to illustrate these strengths, plus demonstrate some knowledge and skill in properties. You will notice that Ben enrolled in property management courses and he sent his resume to several businesses in town who he knew hired persons with administrative and management skills.

Ben had his resume typed on an electric typewriter at a secretarial service. He purchased good quality, heavy buff paper and copied his resume on this paper with a dry copy machine.

Here is Ben's **chronological** resume with a Summary of Qualifications.

PROFESSIONAL PROFILE

BENJAMIN WHITFIELDER

4116 Berry Court
Oxon Hill, Maryland 20021
Home Telephone: (301) 716-1100
Business Answering Service: (301) 998-1610

CAREER OBJECTIVE: To manage properties and use my supervision and human
relations skills to contribute to the overall efficiency of
and operation an apartment complex.

SUMMARY OF
QUALIFICATIONS:
*Managed personnel for a variety of organizations and am known
for effective time and cost saving procedures.

*Prepared, managed, and controlled expenses for annual budgets
up to $500,000.

*Trained supervisors and was recognized for the development
of a program that reduced time and costs by 35%.

*Completely overhauled on-site bookkeeping methods resulting
in better control and elimination of theft problems.

*Controlled a marketing budget totalling over $30,000/month for
advertising, brochures, referrals, and clients.

EDUCATION: Bachelor of Science in Business Administration, 1958, University of Maryland, College Park, Maryland. Major: Business,
Minor: Accounting.

Certificate in Property Management, In Progress, Institute of
Real Estate Management, Laurel, Maryland.

WORK HISTORY: August, 1959 - August, 1978: General Manager, Solo Drug
Company, Landover, Maryland.

May, 1942 - May, 1959: Lieutenant Commander, United States
Navy, Specialized in supply and purchasing.

PERSONAL: Birthdate: April 7, 1924
Health: Excellent
Marital Status: Married, Four children
Interests: Jogging, tennis, fishing.

REFERENCES: Available upon request.

115

MAN/ENGINEER/DESIRES CONSULTING

Case Study #17: Jack C. Sommes

Jack worked with three other persons in an office of a large engineering research firm. Funded mainly by government grants, Jack's whole professional world was working with the same people in a sterile environment with little opportunity for advancement.

He was becoming dissatisfied with this job environment and decided to seek a position with an engineering consulting firm, a firm which would allow him the same salary and benefits plus an opportunity to travel and interact with more people.

Jack's background was in business and engineering. While at his university, he combined engineering and business, then later returned to complete an M.S. degree in Management Technology.

Jack was a technician, and during his military service with the Air Force he was on special assignment with NASA. He was considered to be an expert in Aerospace Technology. He was active in the American Society of Electrical Engineers (ASEE) and the American Society of Consulting Engineers (ASCE).

His problem with his resume was his limited experience in consulting plus lack of opportunity to demonstrate his skills in management and computer technology, although he has skills in both.

Resume Design: Jack had a real resume problem. The one barrier which could keep him from an effective self-presentation was his lack of experience in engineering areas unrelated to space technology.

He did careful research through ASEE and contacts in the consulting business to determine precisely what skill areas were expected by most firms. He also focused on one or two areas basic to all areas of engineering.

He selected skill areas carefully and wrote about his accomplishments in those areas. He also stressed his human relations and communication skills—essential for the consulting business.

Here is Jack's **chronological** resume.

PROFESSIONAL PROFILE

JACK C. SOMMES
911 Dexter Street
San Antonio, Texas 78200

Home Telephone: (512) 412-1611
Business Telephone: (512) 672-7676

CAREER OBJECTIVE: To consult in the area of electrical engineering and to utilize expertise in aerodynamics and construction to create innovative and unique engineering designs.

SUMMARY OF QUALIFICATIONS:

* Innovative and creative talents for the design and development of cost-saving electronic devices.

* Proven competence in both mechanical and electrical engineering concepts.

* Knowledgeable in market data analysis and identifying potential for engineering products and services.

* Skilled in human relations, self-presentations and sales.

* Am a good communicator and am recognized for my ability to identify problems and work toward their solution.

WORK HISTORY:

September 1972 to present: SOUTHWEST RESEARCH INSTITUTE, San Antonio, Texas.

Project Leader

Accountable for the overall management and supervision of project team to include budget preparation, design, and coordination.

August 1969 to September 1972: SOUTHWEST RESEARCH INSTITUTE, San Antonio, Texas

Consulting Engineer

Instrumental in the design and production of hydraulic systems for aero-space construction.

July 1966 to August 1969: MULKEY ENGINEERING, Houston, Texas

Designed and constructed electrolytic components. Responsible for the overall supervision, purchase, and installation of units.

June 1962 to June 1966: UNITED STATES AIR FORCE

Military Service -- honorable discharge.

EDUCATION: Master of Science Degree, 1965, University of Houston, Texas, Houston, Texas. Major: Management Technology, Minor: Administrative Science.

Bachelor of Science Degree, 1962, University of Oklahoma, Norman, Oklahoma. Major: Electrical Engineering, Minor: Business Administration.

Seminar: "The Engineer as Consultant," April, 1978, American Society for Electrical Engineers.

Seminar: "Managing Small Business Enterprises," July, 1977, American Management Association, Dallas, Texas.

RELATED PROFESSIONAL EXPERIENCE:
Member: American Society of Electrical Engineers, 1966 - present.
Regional Director, 1969-70
Regional Coordinator, 1968-69
Member: American Society of Consulting Engineers, 1974 - present
Panel member, "Engineering and Ecstasy," June, 1977, American Society of Consulting Engineers Annual Convention, Denver, Colorado.

PERSONAL INFORMATION:
Birthdate: February 15, 1940
Health: Excellent
Marital Status: Single
Interests: Gourmet Cooking, Ballooning, Sports.

REFERENCES: Available upon requests.

MAN/SALES/DESIRES SALES MANAGEMENT

Case Study #18: Mark Schumann

Most of the case studies presented thus far have focused on people with areas of concern regarding the design of a resume. What about the person who has no particular career or resume problem and would like to design his or her resume to advance in prestige, salary and responsibility?

Mark represents such a case. He is dynamic, energetic, enthusiastic, and has had an outstanding record in sales and marketing. He wants to become a sales manager and feels that he has paid his dues as a sales representative. He wants something different and desires to change organizations.

Resume Design: The design of Mark's resume is rather simple. It is easy to identify his strengths and reflect them on the resume. His work history shows a steady rise in job responsibility, salary, and professional growth.

He selected a confidential resume since he did not want his current employer aware of his job search.

Mark's resume is **chronolgoical** with a Qualifications component.

CONFIDENTIAL PROFESSIONAL PROFILE

MARK A. SCHUMANN

14 Oak Street
South Fork, Illinois 60617
Business: (312) 982-2259
Home: (312) 532-2465

OBJECTIVE: To obtain a Marketing Manager position with a growth-oriented organization in the consumer packaged goods field.

QUALIFICATIONS: Twelve years of management and "hands-on" experience in marketing and sales including:

*Administrative Management
*Marketing Plans
*Sales Promotions
*Sales Techniques Development
*New Product Development
*National Advertising Campaigns
*Sales Forecasting and Quota Setting
*Incentive Programs
*Sales Training
*Personnel Selection

EXPERIENCE:

March 1971 to September 1978: FARBER INDUSTRIES/South Fork, Illinois

Assistant Marketing Manager, Cereal Division and Snacks Division, Kookie-Krisp Cereal and numerous New Products. Additional responsibilities recently received congruent with management's increasing emphasis on new product development. Title promotion promised with new product test market launch. Directly report to Corporate Marketing Manager.

Success Programs

--Executed most successful pre-sweet cereal intro in 12 years
--Successfully developed and introduced 3rd flavor in June 1978
--Brand currently holds a 1.6% SAMI share; 7th in industry
--1978 share potential 2.0%; highest ever for Farber Industries
--Drafted Farber's Pre-Sweet Public Policy Statement
--Successfully developed and executed adult advertising test
--Drafted and executed regional media/promotion opportunity paper.
--Proposed and received approval on major plant expansion project
--Currently executing new end-use strategy
--Currently designing 7 additional volume-building opportunities

September 1971 to April 1975 - Group Product Manager, Cereal Division, Kookie-Krisp Cereal. Total profit-loss ($35MM sales), advertising-promotion ($10MM), market research ($150M), packaging, market and media planning responsibilities. Directly reported to Group Product Manager.

MARK A. SCHUMANN
Confidential Professional Profile
Page Two

Experience (continued)

September 1966 to March 1971: KIMSET COMPANY/Los Angeles, California

Product Manager, Porter Foods Division. Financial responsibilities for product line. Coordinated new marketing programs ... Made seven reports to Chairman.

September 1966 to August 1968 - Assistant Product Manager, Porter Foods Division. Responsible for 7 products in 25 product lines. Coordinated all advertising programs. Worked on three new products.

EDUCATION: MBA, Northwestern University, June 1966, Majors: Marketing and Finance. Concentration in Marketing, Marketing Research, and Advertising. Advanced courses in each taking a total of 11 in three years.

BBA, University of Denver, Denver, Colorado, June 1964. Major: Marketing. Concentration in Marketing and Management. Member of Sigma Alpha Epsilon social fraternity. Held four offices. Business GPA 3.3 of 4.0. Graduated in upper 25% of Denver's BBA class.

PROFESSIONAL ACCOMPLISHMENTS: Recently requested to provide leadership training for Dale Carnegie's Course in Public Speaking and Human Relations. As a May graduate won three awards; Best Speech, Most Improvement, and Highest Achievement in class (1978).

Chosen by Kimset's Head of Corporate Public Relations to lead a team of six Kimset employees as advisors for a Junior Achievement Class in Redondo Beach, California. The JA company, String Illustrated, won monthly sales, production, and attendance awards (1976 to 1977).

PERSONAL: Birthdate: November 22, 1940
Health: Excellent
Interests: Jogging, Tennis, Reading, Writing

REFERENCES: Available upon request.

WOMAN/PRODUCTION MANAGER/ DESIRES EXECUTIVE POSITION

Case Study #19: Susan Fitzgerald

The movement of women into executive positions is a current trend in business and industry. More and more organizations are recognizing the importance of women in management and the significant contribution they can make.

Susan was a talented woman who had made a career in manufacturing. She was unmarried and devoted her time and energy in earning advanced degrees as well as designing and implementing innovative programs to improve efficiency and production for her company.

Her contributions were significant and it was apparent that Susan was being groomed for the position of manager of manufacturing for a large eastern-based firm.

However, Susan perceives some animosity among her male peers and senses that her assuming such a position would create feelings of ill-will and problems for her as an executive.

As these suspicions became confirmed, Susan chose to seek out a similar position with another firm.

Resume Design: Susan had no problem determining accomplishments. Her work indicated that she was capable of making significant contributions to any organization. Her primary barrier was that she was a female production manager who wanted to enter the male-oriented manufacturing manager role.

The resume had to be accomplishment-oriented, and stress professionalism and results.

Determined to be as professional as possible Susan had her resume designed, typeset and printed.

Susan's **chronological** resume is on the following page.

Susan G. Fitzgerald

7560 West Brandenberry Court
Stamford, Connecticut 06905
Home Telephone: (203) 236-6667
Business Telephone: (203) 971-7771

Career Objective:

To make a solid bottom line contribution as a manager of manufacturing for a medium-to-large organization.

Summary of Qualifications:

- Major contributor to the design and implementation of a production system resulting in a 120% reduction of time.
- Created and published first organizational manual for performance reviews and am recognized authority on employee performace ratings.
- Skilled in the design and delivery of innovative learning packages for training employees at all levels.
- Instrumental in negotiating a successful union contract that averted a major shutdown and saved the company over **$1,000,000** in benefits.
- Recognized as sole contributor to the creation and implementation of back up procedures for all major functions within the production department.

Work History:

1975 to present:

AMAX INDUSTRIES/New York, New York
Production Manager

Amax is a major producer of electronic and scientific equipment. The organization is world wide with its headquarters in New York. Accountable to the manufacturing manager and responsibilities range from innovative designs to production flow to development and implementation of personnel policies and practices.

1970 to 1975:

AMAX INDUSTRIES/New York, New York
Assistant Production Manager

Assisted the production manager in developing and implementing cost saving procedures, policies, and employee practices.

1966 to 1970:

MANVILLE CORPORATION/Roxbury, Massachusetts.
Production Supervisor

Manville is heavily involved in the manufacture of synthetic fibers for use in business and industry.

Reported to the production manager and directly responsible for the supervision and direction of 67 employees in a union shop.

1963 to 1966:

MANVILLE CORPORATION/Roxbury, Massachusetts.
Staff Assistant

Assisted in the design and implementation of production policies, procedures, and programs.

Education:

Master of Business Administration, 1976, Harvard Business School, Major: Production Management; Minor: Finance

Bachelor of Science Degree, 1963, Brown University, Major: Business Administration; Minor: Accounting

Related Professional Experience:

Member, American Management Association, 1970 to present
Regional Coordinator, Association of Industrial Managers, 1977 to present, Member, 1972 to present
Recipient, Outstanding Manger, Amax Industries, 1976 to 1977
Presenter, "Negotiating Successful Union Contracts", American Management Association National Conference, April, 1978
Presenter, "Motivating Employees via Performance Review", American Society of Personnel Administrators, Connecticut Chapter, December, 1978
Chapter Contributor, *The Elements of Performance Evaluation*, Howard University Press, to be released, Spring, 1978

Personal:

Birthdate: April 7, 1941
Health: Excellent
Interests: Health, Aviation (own pilot's license), Tennis, Golf

References:

Available Upon Request

MAN/MANUFACTURING EXECUTIVE/ BEING OUTPLACED/DESIRES HIGHER POSITION

Case Study #20: Edward D. Menhalter

Ed was a very competent employee who found himself out of work when his company discontinued their operations in his division and sold the plant to another corporation to raise cash. Since there were no other positions open, the company asked for his resignation. In light of his dedicated employee record, however, they provided him with the services of an executive outplacement firm skilled in helping executives make transitions from one position to another.

Ed took this very hard but determined that it could be the very opportunity he needed to move up to V.P. of Operations at the corporate level, something he had been working towards for years.

Resume Design: Ed's strategy was to use a **chronological** resume with an Accomplishments section to highlight an outstanding track record. In addition, Ed wanted to take a very sophisticated approach and had his resume designed and professionally printed. Also, Ed selected 10½ × 14¼ paper folded once to look like a brochure. It was printed on the front cover and both inside pages.

Here is Ed's resume.

CONFIDENTIAL PROFESSIONAL PROFILE

EDWARD D. MENHALTER

10 So. Allison Way Home: (203) 770-1902
Westport, Connecticut 06880 Answering: (203) 781-5151

OBJECTIVE

Industrial operations management as V.P. of Operations in a medium-to-heavy manufacturing environment.

QUALIFICATIONS

Twelve years professional progressive management responsibilities in the following areas:

General Management
Marketing/Sales
Financial Administration
Planning/Scheduling
Personnel Development
Program Development
Time/Motion Studies

EDUCATION

Master of Business Administration, 1964, University of Southern California/Emphasis in Finance
Bachelor of Science in Mechanical Engineering, 1962, Colorado School of Mines/Golden, Colorado
American Management Association Courses
Management by Objectives, 1966
Art of Negotiating, 1967
Human Relations in Management, 1967
Advanced Industrial Management, 1969, 1970, 1971
Zero Based Budgeting, 1976

PROFESSIONAL ACCOMPLISHMENTS

Have completely revised and implemented purchasing and inventory controls which resulted in a 5–7% savings (total annual amount $300,000) on companies cost of various furnished manufactured goods.

Directly supervised the price control of key industrial goods (inventory value 20 million dollars). Profit margins and inventory turns were increased by 3–5%.

Conducted time-motion studies on several key "bottleneck" production and finishing lines. Studied product infeed systems closely, manufacturing processes and product outfeed. Presented the study to management and shortly thereafter was promoted to Assistant Plant Manger.

Had a direct measurable impact on increased production efficiency by designing and implementing new operations manuals for each production department.

Designed a program to obtain an analysis of those individuals possessing managment potential. This program became the guide for the corporation and was used in all operating divisions to select individuals qualified to fill management positions.

Reorganized the internal operation of the distribution center. This reorganization decreased (25%) the time required to process internal paper work

Designed a scheduling system for production, inventory control, maintenance, and quality control (Briefing Board Concept). This system increased efficiency 20% in the department and also improved the morale of personnel.

Directed personnel in handling credit procedures and truck schedules. The efficiency of deliveries was improved and all personnel became more aware of accounts which were credit risks.

Supervised all operations while Production Superintendent for the mill equipment remanufacturing department. A production increase of 200–300% was made in one product line

PROFESSIONAL EXPERIENCE

PLANT MANAGER/East Coast Industries, Westport, Connecticut. Total profit and loss responsibility for this industrial manufacturing facility. Total sales of light industrial goods are 50 million dollars. Increased sales by 57 percent over a five year period. Significantly improved profit margins and reduced cost margin of producing product. (1973 to 1978)

ASSISTANT PLANT MANAGER/Fabricators, Inc., Toledo, Ohio. Responsibilities included financial, sales, and manufacturing of light and heavy machinery, industrial kilns, ball mills, classifiers and crushers. Responsibilities also included management of the steel fabrication shop, assembly department, personnel and customer and union contracts. (1970 to 1973)

MANAGER OF MANUFACTURING/Medium Industries, Inc., Chicago, Illinois. Responsible for all cost centers, machine shop, steel fabrication shop, steel and ductile iron foundry. Supervised shipping and receiving, warehouse and stores, material control, plant engineering, product control, scheduling and quality assurance. (1964 to 1970)

GROUP PRODUCT MANAGER/1966 to 1976
PURCHASING MANAGER, Quality Control/1964 to 1966

AWARDS/PUBLICATIONS/MEMBERSHIPS

American Management Association
Association of Manufacturing Executives, Treasurer of State Chapter, 1969
Association of Purchasing Mangers
AMA Award for high achievement excellence
Award for outstanding contribution to purchasing professionalism
Published: "Managing Manufacturing in the 70's," Industry Magazine, May, 1970

PERSONAL

Age 38 Married Health: Excellent

11

How to Lay Out, Edit, Type, Copy, Select Paper

Do Not Fold, Spindle, or Mutilate

Well you've done it. You have broken your resume into *eight* component parts, looked at formats, and seen what others have done with those formats.

You now have a lot of information about yourself—your interests, goals, and skills. Now it's time to put all of that information into something *meaningful, professional, and dynamic.*

LAYOUT

Strengths First Layout, as we have demonstrated, is critical for a resume. The eight component parts you have assembled need to be arranged in an order which *maximizes* your strengths.

Quickly review each part to see what you have written. Then begin thinking how you can organize them. In terms of Layout, we recommend that on the first attempt you stay close to the illustrations and examples provided. We feel these formats provide ease in reading, are logical and professional, and provide a crisp, clean appearance. Later you can make your own adaptations.

White Space In addition, resume writers often talk about **White Space.** This concept refers to the amount of margins and spacing between components and paragraphs. Generally, the more white space you have the easier it is to read!

The eye can flow from one component to another with ease, and it helps reduce reading time (greatly appreciated by most employers).

The **Layout** process involves taking each component part and arranging it on a piece of paper. You may want to take scissors and cut out each part and then tape it to a blank sheet of paper in the order which *you* feel will have the greatest impact.

Criteria The criteria for effective Layout are:

* Readability
  * Plenty of White Space
    * Uncrowded
      * Strengths are always toward the front (of the first page) of the resume, with less important information indicated on the second page
        * Limit resume to two pages

EDITING

A person who uses a great many words to express
his meaning is like a bad marksman who instead of
aiming a single stone at an object takes up a
handful and throws at it in hopes he may hit.
—*Samuel Johnson*

Johnson is saying that it is better to select words that will pinpoint your meaning rather than be too wordy and not get the point across.

You probably have enough information from your worksheets to compile two resumes. **Editing** is the process of taking all this information and condensing it into a readable document. It also means building *sell* into the resume.

Tips   Here are tips to assist you in Editing the information you have:

* Expand your *recent experience* (particularly if it is related to the Career Objective).

    * *Minimize repetition,* particularly in the Work History component. For example, there is no need to repeat yourself if you have already discussed your skills in the Experience paragraph.

        * *Combine* high school and college part-time work experiences in order to save space.

If you have a college degree, it is not necessary to list a high school diploma.

           * Write in a *logical, orderly sequence.* In the Experience paragraph, for instance, write the overall skill areas first, such as Administering and Managing; then proceed to specific skill areas, such as Designing, Illustrating, or Researching.

               * Wherever possible *use sell words* that make an *impact* on the reader. Refer to the list in Chapter Three to select ACTION words.

PAPER SELECTION

Classic laid, Rice, Water-marked, parchment, weaved—these aren't secret recipe formulas; these are the various kinds of paper you can choose from, which could be the key to an outstanding resume.

Criteria   The criteria for Paper Selection are:

* Style of paper
    * Color
        * Weight
           * Cost

These styles can be specified when printing your resume or can be purchased from a printer or paper distributor for use with dry copier machines. Check the Yellow Pages to find printers and paper suppliers; shop around, because prices will vary.

Color   When selecting paper colors remember that your resume is not modern art. Select paper that looks *sophisticated and professional.*

Usually, colors like greys, buffs, ivory, light blue, light brown, or white are excellent.

Weight   The weight of the paper is related to its stiffness. *Heavy paper* can result in a more unique, crisp, and attention-getting resume. You may want to see samples at your printer.

TYPING, PRINTING, OR COPYING?

Tips: Original typing of the resume should be done on an *electric typewriter* with a correcting feature to cleanly erase any mistakes.

In addition, if you are printing from the typed original *use correction fluid* to clean up smudges and other imperfections.

Type style should be *clean and professional.* Spacing (whether 10 or 12 characters per inch) should be selected depending on the length of the resume.

Here are some standard Typing Styles found in most offices:

```
IBM ADVOCATE type is an open spaced square-serif design.
IBM COURIER 72 type is a square-serif design in the Pica
family of type styles.
IBM DELEGATE type is a weighted type conveying the feel-
ing of printed material.
IBM PRESTIGE PICA 72 type is similar to Prestige Pica
type style offered with the IBM Model D Typewriter.
IBM LETTER GOTHIC type is a distinctive sans-serif design.
```

The issue of whether to type each resume or have it printed is a matter of personal choice. Either one produces a professional-looking resume and both are acceptable to employers. If you have the time and money, and can contract with a professional printer, do so. However, if you are on a shoe-string budget or need a resume quickly, then type it and make copies on a quality dry copy machine.

There are three ways to finish your resume:

  * type each copy separately

    * print it in quantities

      * make copies on a dry copy machine

Let's look at these one at a time.

Typing Each Copy

Personal Quality   This method can be effective when your job search is limited and you are seeking only a few interviews. It adds a personal touch; however, it is not recommended for extensive mailings.

Printing

Large Mailing   Typing a master copy, proofing it, and sending it to a printer for a large quantity of resumes is preferred by some people. If your job search calls for a massive mailing then use a printer.

  DO NOT FOLD, SPINDLE OR MUTILATE

It is a good idea to order 100 or so extra blank sheets of paper to make copies on a dry copy machine should you choose to modify your resume or if you need only a few copies for a special job opening.

Copying

Low Cost

Printing does not allow the flexibility of using a dry copy machine. If you feel that you won't be needing more than 100 to 150 copies of your resume we suggest a copy machine.

With a good machine the copies appear as if they have been printed, especially if you copy your resume on the heavier paper styles recommended earlier.

The advantage is: You have a professional appearing resume at a low cost with the flexibility to tailor-make resumes for specific job openings. Be sure to retain a clean, white, typed master.

LETTERHEAD, ENVELOPES, AND
BUSINESS CARDS

An added personal touch preferred by some people is the purchase of letterhead, envelopes, and business cards.

Some people obtain letterhead in the same color as their resume, while others use unique designs. It is a matter of personal taste.

Business cards (particularly if you're unemployed) adds a professional touch if you meet people at coffees, professional association meetings, or seminars.

Worth It! These methods may seem expensive to you; however, the investment can pay off in getting the right kind of job with the right kind of salary.

R E S U M E   A C T I O N   S T E P

Putting It All Together

Objective: To write your resume.

Materials: Pencil and paper
Tape and scissors
Eight components of The Resume Experience.

Action Steps: 1. Reread the components you have completed and assemble them in the sequence which best sells your strengths to an employer.

2. Edit the material to fit a two page resume.

3. Rewrite the material in resume style. Take into account layout, white space, ease of reading, action words, and the like.

4. Have someone read the resume for critical feedback and further editing.

5. Retype the resume for copying and/or printing. Be certain to proof your final copy for errors.

6. Determine quantity and paper style.

Congratulations! You have now completed The Resume Experience! Now turn to Chapter 12, "Beyond The Resume Experience" for a discussion of special situations and unusual resumes.

12

Special Situations and
Unusual Resumes

Beyond the Resume Experience

Generally, the guidelines for resume preparation call for a conservative and professional approach. Many employers are wary of unusual or far out approaches which project a person who is too progressive, too aggressive, difficult to work with, or who is compensating for an insecurity in their personality.

On the other hand, some employers are looking for the unusual and creative person, the person who will go "the extra mile" to gain attention. This type of employer is in the minority; however, there are organizations where this approach will work.

Special Situations: There are some occupations and career fields that allow for creating an unusual resume. Typically, people in these occupations are creative and are expected to do the unusual. Artists, writers, illustrators, fashion designers, interior designers, graphics specialists, advertising executives, and marketing specialists, are some examples.

A word of caution: If you decide to try an unusual resume be certain to research the organization first to be sure your efforts will be appreciated!

UNUSUAL RESUME FORMATS

You name it and somewhere a resume writer has tried it! Examples are:

* Leather Bound
  * French-fold
    * Book Style
      * Brochure Style
        * Mini-Portfolios
          * Covers and Spiral Bound
            * Photographs
          * Letters of Introduction
        * Resume on a Billboard
      * Documents and Reference Letters Attached
    * Oversized
  * Undersized
* Self-mailers
  * Mailgrams
    * Audio Cassette Tapes
      * Autobiographical Style

We even heard of one job seeker who sent his resume in a shoe box with an old shoe. A letter of introduction stated "Now that I've got my shoe in the door, how about an interview!"

All of these approaches have their own advantages and disadvantages and require careful consideration as to design, approach, and strategy. Let's discuss some of these approaches in greater detail.

Mini-Portfolio

If you are an artist, graphics specialist, illustrator, or writer, you may wish to design your resume around samples of your work.

The approach is to begin with the usual components, such as Heading And Identification, Accomplishments, Work History, and so on, and then proceed to a collage of your work samples.

Note: One important consideration is that the reproduction, reductions, layout, and process necessary to bring the resume to "camera ready" status for printing can be costly.

Brochure Style

One variation is to have your resume printed on an 11″ by 17″ sheet of quality paper, and then fold each copy once to the size of an 8½″ by 11″ letter.

Your resume then opens and reads like a brochure about you. Typically, the first page is an introduction of you. For instance:

R E S U M E

for

KATHRYN J. WRIGHT

Or CONFIDENTIAL PROFESSIONAL PROFILE

KATHRYN J. WRIGHT

The inside pages are organized with the components which best sell you. Unless you have a lengthy resume the back page is usually left blank.

Another variation of this approach is to fold the resume into a Self-Mailer by stapling the ends and using the blank back page for the address.

Photographs?

Usually Not

A question frequently asked by resume writers is whether or not they should include a photograph of themselves.

For most situations the answer is to omit the photograph. If you are in the technical fields, such as data processing, accounting, or engineering, the organization isn't interested in *what* you look like but in your ability to do the job.

Exception

On the other hand: If you are in sales, marketing, or public relations, and wish to work for an organization where you know *image* is of paramount importance, and you have the kind of *image* they want, then you may wish to include a photograph.

If included, the photograph is part of the Heading And Identification component and should appear either right or left of center depending on the format of the name and address component.

Caution!

As a final note, you should be aware that some employers are wary of persons who try to make an impression based on their looks.

Book Style

An interesting variation is to create a small book about yourself by taking three sheets of 8½″ by 11″ paper and folding them in half.

The three sheets are then stapled at the fold creating the book. The front cover is the introduction page and the remaining pages tell your story using the eight components of The Resume Experience.

Spiral Bound

A resume can be given a polished look by covering it with hard poster board paper then binding it with a spiral. Most printing shops have a spiral binder punch and plastic binders. Again, expense should be a consideration.

French-Fold

Place your resume on a larger piece of colored paper so that the colored paper forms a border around your resume.

Then fold over the top portion of the colored border and staple it to the resume. This creates a "report" style format which can be very attractive and professional.

When using this style it is better to mail the resume in a large envelope to avoid folding it.

The Key   As you can see, there are many alternatives to using unusual resumes. We have touched on only a few and leave it to your creative or conservative judgement. The key is to make certain your resume has a style which fits you and the organization you are applying to. An unusual resume will get attention and could be a quick path to concluding a successful job search.

Now That You've Got It, What Are You Going to Do With It?

See, the conquering hero comes,
Sound the trumpets, beat the drums.
—Thomas Morell

Well, now that you have your resume what are you going to do with it? File it? Show it to your mother? Pass it out at weddings? Hang it on the wall? Or are you going to get a job that fits the kind of person you represented on those two sheets of paper?

Whatever your reason for spending an evening with The Resume Experience, we feel it's appropriate to provide some basic tips on how you can *use* the resume to uncover job leads. In Part Two our intent is not to provide a comprehensive job search strategy, but to give you some basic hints on how the Resume, as a job search and career planning tool, can be your best friend in getting the right job.

As a reminder, here are several good reasons for having a resume:

* *Uncover Job Leads* One of the more obvious and rewarding purposes of a resume is to uncover job leads. The idea is to get your piece of advertising into as many hands as possible. In the job search business this activity is called "gaining visibility." The next step is to tell each recipient of your resume the reason he or she has it, and that you would appreciate a chance to sit down and discuss opportunities, leads, or referrals with persons who might be able to assist you.

  * *The Interview* Your resume also assists in marketing you prior to and during an interview. Often an interviewer works directly from a resume during the interview. Naturally a well-organized and written resume will *facilitate* the process considerably. Not only is the interviewer hearing positive things about you, he or she is also seeing your positive strengths on the resume.

    * *Post-Interview Selling* Actually, this isn't as technical as it sounds. One of the primary reasons for a resume is to represent you in an employer's office *after* the interview. In a tight race for the position between you and another person, the resume may make the difference. As the final hiring authority continues to mull over the decision your resume is being read over and over, by several people. This is why it is a good idea to customize your resume to the specific opportunity — the resume then continues to be your sales representative.

ACTION FORM LETTERS

Many veteran job seekers have said that "getting a job is a hard job." We agree and feel that any tool or resource we can provide to assist you in the process will be welcome.

It is hard enough to keep it all together during an extensive job search without having to create from scratch all of the various correspondence you will need in order to make your search successful. To assist you we have included a complete section of letters which can be plugged into a variety of situations. In addition, the samples will guide you in creating your own letters. These Action Form Letters are contained in Chapter 14 of Part Two.

13

Some Creative Ways to Uncover Job Leads

Resume Uses and Abuses

DIRECT MAIL—SHOOT WITH A RIFLE, NOT A SHOTGUN

In this day and age there is little one can do inexpensively. So it goes with the job search. The cost of everything—printing, postage, gas, clothes, directories, business and professional periodicals, telephones, and on and on—has gone up.

The Direct Mail method is expensive but can be the most effective and fastest way to find the right job. So don't just blindly mail hundreds of resumes in all directions; rather, mail it to a specific person with some type of follow up strategy.

Question: So where do I find these names and job leads?

Answer: Good question. Actually, there are numerous areas and resources for names of persons who could assist you. Before that, however, consider this approach: There doesn't have to be an actual job opening before you can contact an individual in an organization. You are researching, getting information, referrals, job leads. Even if each contact provides you with only one lead, you are on your way. This approach is not as difficult as it may seem. Although we will discuss it later, all these strategies require that you *stick with it*—try the technique, get burned a couple of times, feel awkward perhaps, but continue trying the techniques. Believe us—they work!

Now to answer your question: where do you find the names and uncover job leads? The following is not a complete list, but it will get you started in the right direction:

Limited Possibilities

Classified Ads. This has long been the place where most job seekers go first. The limitations are that very few mid- to high-level jobs get listed. In addition, the response and competition can be fierce.

Read Between The Lines

Periodicals. The business sections of newspapers, professional journals, newsletters, and other professional publications can open up a whole host of job opportunities. Read between the lines. For example, articles on promotions, companies relocating, new products, or funding sources can spell *opportunity*. Why not research the opportunity by sending your resume and then follow-up with a request for an interview to further learn about the organization.

Contacts   *Business Cards.* Collecting business cards—old or new ones—provides a good source of names, addresses, and telephone numbers. Ask your friends to lend you theirs. This simple practice can provide a wealth of contacts.

Be Visible!   *Association Member Lists.* Professional associations are useful whether you're staying in your career or not. Attending meetings as a guest or becoming a member provides you with a wealth of names for lining up potential interviews and for uncovering influential contacts. Becoming visible among your professional peers is an excellent job-seeking strategy.

Additional Sources. Besides the ones listed, the following are additional sources to consider:

* Former professors
    * Business associates
        * Other job seekers
            * College alumni
                * Community leaders
                    * Department Heads
* Personnel Directories
    * Former employers and co-workers
        * Friends
            * Clergy
                * Company Officers
                    * Supervisors

Except in the case of the Letter Resume, a Cover Letter should accompany all resumes. See Chapter 14 for tips on Cover Letter design.

Mechanics of the Direct Mail

Get ready for a Cardinal Rule: *All Cover Letters must be typed.* This can be done one at a time, or with large mailings you may want to contract with a secretarial service to have the cover letter auto-typed. You may even want the letter printed for large mailings.

It is important that the letter appears to be an "original" and that you sign each one individually. There is nothing worse than an employer receiving a "form" letter from a job seeker.

The best practice is to limit the amount of your direct mail to the amount of *follow-up* interviews you can arrange within ten days of mailing. After all, it is the personal contact you make with each person which will generate the most job-leads, contacts, referrals, and offers!

Be aware also that the persons you send your resume to will often get behind on their mail because they are either busy, out of town, or in meetings. It is necessary to allow some compensation time-wise. Probably a mailing of fifteen to twenty resumes per day will keep you occupied with follow-ups.

Finally, it is crucial to keep *up-to-date* records of where the mailings were sent, when, and to whom. Unless you have a mind like a steel trap you can easily lose track of mailings and contacts, and possibly lose some good leads. A simple chart with the following headings would help:

* Date Mailed
    * To Whom (include address)
        * Date To Follow-Up
          * Date of Interview
            * Follow-Up Action

Direct Mail Follow-up—Asking For The Interview

Using this technique is similar to other first-time experiences—It's *scary!*

It's like going to an employment agency for the first time, or going through a first interview experience, or like the new salesperson making a first call while learning how to use the telephone for a sales presentation.

Whatever the experience, you will need to go through it several times before becoming proficient and comfortable.

The following is a *step by step* procedure to use in asking for an interview following a direct mail campaign. Included with the steps are examples of telephone conversations.

Get a Name   *Step One.* Get the name of someone within an organization where you would like to work or who deals with the type of career field you seek.

Or, let's assume you do not know the name of a person within the organization; let's say this is an organization where you want to do some career research and possibly uncover or create a job opportunity. Here's how you get a specific name to send your resume to:

(Phone rings)

Receptionist: Corland Industries—May I help you?

You: Yes. I'm sending some material to your manager of manu-facturing but I don't have a name; could you help me please?

Receptionist: Just one moment please. Yes, that name is Fred Jones and his correct title is "Production Manager."

You: Thank you for your help.

Question: Is it this easy every time to get names from organizations?

Answer: Most of the time, but not always. They may not understand who it is you are calling for, or they may ask what it is you are sending. Rather than asking for someone by title you may have to ask for a particular department and then ask the secretary/receptionist in that department for the name.

Be sure to be assertive, and roleplay what you are going to say before making the call.

If you are not sure who to send your resume to, or if you perhaps want to first talk to someone who may know of overall opportunities in the organization, call and get the name of the Director of Personnel or someone in that department.

Mail, Then Telephone

Step Two: Mail your resume with an attached cover letter and make a follow-up phone call.

Allow two days for the mail to be delivered if the organization is local. An out-of-state location usually requires three to seven days.

Be Prepared!

A critical mistake made by most job seekers is that they are unprepared for many responses which arise when making a follow-up telephone call! For example, your contact may not have read the mail, or maybe they put your correspondence aside to look at sometime in the future.

In another instance the person may have read your letter, passed it on to the Personnel Department and then completely forgot about it. Finally, if your contact is out of town or in a meeting, you must be prepared to leave a message.

Message Rule:

The rule to remember concerning messages is this: don't leave a message unless you feel it is necessary. The reason is that *you* want to control the situation—you don't want this person to call you when you're off-guard. In addition, it's possible that the person will not return your call and you will wind up leaving several messages. Then your chances of getting through worsen because you create the image of being a pest.

Consider the following illustration of a telephone follow-up to a cover letter and resume:

(Phone rings)

Receptionist: Corland Industries—May I help you?

Barbara: Yes, I need to speak with Mr. Fred Jones. By the way, I'll be calling back again; does he have a direct number?

Receptionist: Yes, that number is 755-2120. I'll connect you.

(Pause)

Secretary: Mr. Jones' office—May I help you?

Barbara: Yes, this is Barbara. Is Fred in? I need to talk with him about some materials. Could you put me right through please?

Secretary: What is the nature of your business, Barbara?

Barbara: I'm currently involved in some research. Fred would be of real assistance with this, could you put me through please?

Secretary: Ah, er, yes, just one moment.

Fred: Fred Jones, may I help you?

Barbara: Yes, Mr. Jones, this is Barbara Hankins and the reason I called is that I'm currently involved in some research and thought maybe you could help.

Fred: What can I do for you, Barbara?

Barbara: Well Fred, I recently sent you a letter with a synopsis of my background. Has it made it to your desk yet?

Fred: Barbara Hankins. Hankins. Ah yes, here it is. Gee, I remember looking at it. Your background is excellent . . . but we currently don't have any openings.

Barbara: Mr. Jones, when I sent you that letter, I anticipated that you wouldn't have any immediate openings. But as I said earlier, I'm really doing some research on a variety of career alternatives.

I don't want to do what so many others have done and wind up on a dead-end job, underemployed, or unhappy in my work. I would like to know more about your industry, your company, and what you do. I only need 15 minutes or so. Would it be possible to see you next week?

Fred: Well, I'm not sure I can help, but sure! Let's get together next Tuesday, about 2:00 p.m. O.K?

Barbara: Fine. I'll see you then.

Question: Well, that went smoothly! What about the tough ones?

Answer: Let's take a look at some tough ones; but before we do that, there is an important point in that last illustration. The reason for asking for Fred Jones' telephone number is: In case the secretary doesn't let Barbara through she can call back on the direct line right after working hours or just before work hours—times when the secretary is usually not in. Chances are that Fred is working early or late to get things organized or, like most managers, to get caught up.

Secretary Detours
The following are typical secretary detours, and ways to get around them:

Secretary: Mr. Jones is in a meeting. Can I take a message and have him return the call?

Barbara: Gee, I'm going to be away from the phone. If you can give me a time when he's normally in I'll call then.

Or *Secretary:* What kind of research is it? Maybe I can assist you! Mr. Jones is very busy.

Barbara: Well, it's rather involved—concerning the manufacturing industry, various problems I am experiencing, plus situations with XYZ Industries specifically. Fred would be the best source. If I could speak with him for a few moments, it would help. Thank you.

Or *Secretary:* Does Mr. Jones know you?

Barbara: No, not personally. His name came up in a conversation where it was suggested he could assist me. Could you put me through please?

Or *Secretary:* Barbara, could I have your last name please?

Barbara: Yes, it's Hankins, Barbara Hankins.

Secretary: Oh, Barbara Hankins. I saw your letter and resume. All of our hiring is done through personnel. I'm afraid Mr. Jones would not be able to help you.

Barbara: Well, actually I wasn't applying for a position. I'm currently involved in a research project that would only involve a few minutes of Mr. Jones' time. He's the only one who would be able to answer my questions. Could I speak with him for a few minutes please?

Persistence and Practice
Although these illustrations are simulated, with a little *persistence* and *practice* you will find more and more interviews coming your way.

This technique puts the *control* of the job search into *your* hands and not in the hands of a secretary, receptionist, employment agency, the classified ads, or anything or anybody else who could care less about you and your career.

If the Personnel Department is the only hiring authority for a particular organization, then use the above strategies to see the key persons there.

Step Three: Do a Career Information Interview.

Question: That's a new term. What does it mean?

Answer: It's simply a way to do career and organizational research. **Career Research** determines whether a career is right for you, and **Organization Research** tells you whether a particular organization is right. It also uncovers job leads, contacts, and helps you *create* a job for yourself.

Do Your Homework The key is: Do some quick research on the organization and/or industry before the interview. The more knowledgeable you are, the better you can control the interview and sell your skills, abilities, and problem-solving capabilities.

Read everything you can about the organization, including annual reports, product literature, news releases, and organizational literature.

Here are some helpful "starters" to get the interview going:

* "Well, Mr. Jones, I should start by asking you to give me a brief rundown on your organization, the industry, and your position. What do you do? How did you get to where you are?"

   * "I once faced a problem like that; as a matter of fact, I handled it very much the same way by. . . ."

      * "What would you say are the main problems of the industry?"

         * "Do all organizations in the industry face the same kinds of problems?"

            * "What are your plans for growth over the next two to three years?"

               * "What is the turnover rate among first and second line supervisors?"

                  * "What can I do to become better prepared to join an organization like yours?"

* "Where do I go from here? Do you have any contacts I could talk to? Do you know of any other openings?"

   * "Do you see any way that I might fit into your organization?"

      * "Are you budgeted for additional personnel in the near future?"

There are many more examples, but these give you an idea of how to get the conversation off the ground. Be sure to express

145   RESUME USES AND ABUSES

your appreciation for the interview and ask if you can check back periodically.

Note: This step is important in that successful career changers and job-seekers *all* report that follow-up calls and written communications were *key* ingredients to their success.

Another important aspect of follow-up is to send thank you letters. In these letters, you once again request referrals and assistance.

Sending another mailing to organizations which did not respond or to persons you were unable to reach on the telephone, is another part of good follow-up.

Be selective, since each mailing costs you money; however, it does increase your chances of getting a response.

USING THE RESUME IN THE INTERVIEW

Previously we have suggested that you should feel *comfortable* with your resume and statements it makes about you.

Also, you should be aware of the *impact* your resume makes, particularly if it is written in a dynamic and forceful manner.

To use the resume successfully in an interview, you should relate the information in *an assertive and convincing manner.*

Helpful Hints   Discussing interviewing skills is beyond the scope of this book; however, here are some helpful hints for the interview:

* From your resume, list all of your positive and negative attributes in relation to the job opening. Then, role-play responses which will *sell* your positives and turn your negatives into positives.

  * In role-playing responses, have a friend play the employer and continue practicing until you are comfortable with almost any question.

    * Write out your response to questions prior to the role-play.

      * Remain in control of the interview by fielding questions then asking some *prepared* questions of your own.

The Stress Question

Perhaps the most difficult experience encountered during an employment interview is the Stress Question. Designed to "put you on the spot," the Stress Question analyzes your handling of the question. If you're positive and creative you're a success. However, if your response is nervous, stuttering, and demonstrates a lack of confidence, you may have lost an opportunity.

Preparation for Stress Questions is critical. Although you

Handling Them cannot predict the exact nature of the question, there are strategies available to use in handling it. For example:

* Research possible stress questions by asking peers, former employers, or job seekers who have interviewed with the same organization.
    * Write out answers to possible stress questions. Then record the answers on audio-tape and critique their effectiveness.

Here are some illustrations of Stress Questions, their purposes, and recommended responses:*

STRESS QUESTION	PURPOSE	RESPONSE
1. What are your long-range objectives?	To identify the thought behind your career planning—your ambition—your desire to stay with the organization.	Avoid being vague. Identify your career objective and state it clearly and precisely. Mention the challenge of the position and its relation to your career objective.
2. Why did your leave your last position?	To identify any problems with your previous employer, if you over-stepped the bounds of your position, personality conflicts, or if you were incompetent.	Avoid down-grading a former employer. Prepare a statement which focuses on your desire to learn new skills and seek new opportunities. Avoid details such as salary, work time, prestige, or co-workers.
3. Why should we hire you?	To identify a reason why you should or should not be hired in comparison with other candidates.	Stress your experience, particularly in relation to the career field. Focus on your positive characteristics and indicate that the position would provide the most creative opportunity to improve your career.
4. What is your biggest strength? What is your biggest weakness?	To identify how well you know yourself and your strengths and weaknesses as related to your work experience.	Recognize that all persons have strengths and weaknesses. From the self-assessment, identify your areas. Support your strengths with examples and turn your weaknesses into positives. Keep all examples geared to your business life.

*John E. McLaughlin and Stephen K. Merman, *Sound Advice for Job and Career Strategists* (Denver, Colorado: Portland Management Group, 1977), SG 7, pp. 14–17.

STRESS QUESTION	PURPOSE	RESPONSE
5. Why aren't you earning more at your age?	To identify any feelings of regrets, any grudges, any negative aspect of your personality.	The best response is to tie the answer into your total career plan. You accepted low-paying jobs to gain experience and to develop skills. These positions provided extensive learning experiences.
6. What are your salary requirements?	To identify your feelings regarding your worth.	From your Corporate/Organization Research and other information, identify a realistic salary range.
7. How well do you operate under pressure?	To assess your strengths or to identify situations in your background where you were either successful or unsuccessful in a stress situation.	Formulate an answer which indicates that you operate at peak performance under stress. Cite examples of your performance under stress. Answer this way only if you can perform well in stress situations.
8. Why do you want to work for this particular organization?	To identify if you understand their organization, and if you can sell yourself.	This is a good way to demonstrate your knowledge of the organization from the Corporate/Organization research you completed prior to the interview. Indicate where your skills would be most beneficial in meeting the needs of the organization.
9. What other organizations are you considering?	To identify your marketability—what kind of a "prize" you would be, and how much you have been offered.	Respond that you have interviewed several organizations and name a few of them. If you have interviewed these organizations for information, you may mention them. Be honest and positive in your response.
10. Why did you have so many jobs in the past ten years?	To identify weaknesses, immaturity, a person yet unsettled.	Respond that each change was necessary for your total career plan and growth. Each job provided the kind of opportunity that would develop skills and give different exposure to the career field. Provide examples of each and its contribution to your career.

Remember: thorough preparation pays off during the interview by insuring a confident, self-assured job applicant. Don't interview until you have prepared completely!

Here are a list of common stress questions:

* Are you creative? give an example?
   * What is your philosophy of management?
      * Why are you leaving your present organization?
         * List your five greatest achievements.
            * How have you demonstrated leadership skills.
               * How long would it take you to make a significant contribution to our organization?

* Are you analytical? Give an example.
   * What do you perceive as your major personality strength?
      * How do your peers perceive you?
         * What have your subordinates thought of you?
            * What can you do for this organization that someone else couldn't do?
               * If you had your choice of any position in our organization what would it be?

* If you could begin your career again what would you do differently?
   * Are you interested in serving mankind, or is money your primary motivation?
      * What types of people seem to "rub" you the wrong way?
         * What should a person possess in order to be successful in an organization such as ours?
            * What factors determine a person's progress within an organization?
               * What job in our organization do you want to work toward?

THE RESUME AND THE APPLICATION

Most organizations require that you complete an Employment Application Form. Generally it is completed after you have been offered a position, but at times it is completed as part of the interview process.

Almost all employment applications are only tools for gathering information. They allow little opportunity to express your *positive* skill areas or to discuss the *positive* you.

For this reason it is important to attach a copy of your resume to the employment application. Since the resume is a *marketing* tool, anywhere you can make it visible will help.

Remember: your resume is your partner. Bring a copy to all interviews including the second or third. You may be seeing someone different, or your resume might have been misplaced. Some job-seekers even mail another copy of the resume with interview follow-up letters or general thank-you letters. Memory joggers can't hurt!

THE RESUME AND EMPLOYMENT AGENCIES

We've all been there at one time or another—fighting the crowds, signing our paychecks away, and hoping to get that magic interview and job. Even with the negatives, employment agencies continue to grow at a rapid rate. They survive because job hunters continue to flock to agencies by the thousands each year.

Yet less than 10 percent of these people ever get placed by employment agencies. The reason is that each placement takes a great amount of time to complete, and since most agencies simply aren't staffed to assist *every* person, they only work on those who are the *most marketable now!* The rest, unfortunately, are kept on the string with the old response: "Yes, I'm working on it. These things take time, you know. Check back next week. Ok?"

So you wait for the magic phone call and waste time, money, and energy.

Here's How: The resume then, is a tool for representing the *marketable* you to employment agencies. Here is how to make the best use of them:

* To save valuable time and avoid duplication, find out which are the best agencies in your area for your career field.

  * Ask for an *experienced* employment counselor. One who has been there for more than six months and specializes in your career field.

    * Take a critical look at yourself and your marketability. Upgrade your image in order to make the agency work for you.

      * Most employment agencies require that you fill out their application form, plus sign an agreement regarding employment fees. Sometimes you can short cut this process by writing on the form that you will only accept interviews with fee paid companies. Then sign the form and attach your resume. Be positive and assertive when you do this!

        * Most importantly, quickly recognize when the agency is giving you the runaround or is not working on your placement. The

guideline is that if the agency has not provided any leads or interviews within one and a half weeks, then chances are your employment counselor is working to place more marketable candidates. The key is to follow-up frequently, mail your resume every two weeks to the agency as a reminder, and continue to employ other job-search strategies.

THE RESUME AND RECRUITING FIRMS

Executive recruiting firms—sometimes known as head hunters—work just the opposite from employment agencies.

Employment agencies try to *place* people who come to them for employment help, while executive recruiters have the job assignment from an organization first, then try to head hunt the candidate from a competitor or similar business.

Send Your Resume

Recruiters rarely seek persons who are beginning job-seekers, unemployed, changing careers, or have serious barriers to employment in their resumes. They do not "find jobs for you," but when they get an assignment, they go to their resume files to identify a potential candidate to recruit. For this reason it is important to register yourself with recruiters by sending them your resume.

Remind Them

Also, when you are employed you should update your resume with some recruiting firms each year. You never know when you may become the right candidate for a lucrative opportunity.

A Final Word: Using your resume to creatively uncover job leads is important. Remember that only one in every five jobs is advertised, or listed with employment agencies or search firms. This simple statistic illustrates that uncovering solid job leads is a difficult challenge. Still, it is a challenge you can meet effectively.

Success Follows

Jobs are there for the dynamic, energetic, hard-working career strategist who is willing to spend the time and effort necessary to seek them out! Furthermore, the strategist who is willing to manage his or her career in the most relevant and meaningful way will succeed!

14

Action Letters
That Get Jobs

Creative Covers

The importance of *positive* and *creative* correspondence with potential employers has been stressed throughout The Resume Experience.

To aid the job-seeker in developing his or her personal correspondence this chapter provides a series of easy-reference Action Form Letters.* These letters are designed so that key words, phrases, and paragraphs, are *interchangeable* in order to create a letter which can best represent *you* and generate interest on the part of the employer.

Four Types   This chapter is divided into four general parts:

* *Job-Lead Development Letters, Section A*—Designed specifically to uncover job leads and develop interviews. Some of these letters appear in other sections to illustrate that a Job-Lead letter can also serve as a Thank You/Follow-Up letter. Its specific purpose depends on the job-seeker and his or her particular situation.

  * *Thank You and Interview Follow-Up Letters, Section B*—These letters express appreciation for the person's time and interest. They can be used to create and maintain centers of influence. For example, an appreciation for an interview designed to generate career information could also create a very useful influential contact.

    * *Creating and Maintaining Influential Contacts, Section C*—These letters not only express appreciation, they also identify key persons, organizations or associations which might be beneficial to the job-seeker. They are not specifically designed to uncover job leads—although this could happen. For example, a letter rejecting a job offer could be intentionally worded to maintain that person as an influential contact. After all, you may need that person if the new job doesn't pan out.

      * *Corporate/Organizational Research Letters, Section D*—Letters designed to obtain information about corporations or organizations. These include letters to banks, chambers of commerce, libraries, research centers, and associations. Generally, these letters do not seek information on job openings or any job-seeking advice. They are simply letters requesting information.

Each section is organized in the following manner:

* Each Form Letter is assigned a number.

  * The purpose of the number is to allow for easy reproduction by secretarial services or typing services. For example, letters sent for Corporate/Organizational Research may be similar for any number of organizations. The job-seeker simply instructs the secretarial service to type "letter number D1" and duplicate the letters for a mailing to twenty organizations.

    * To customize a creative letter, expressing *your* uniqueness, merely draw positive and appropriate phrases from various letters and integrate them into one letter.

      *Adapted from: John E. McLaughlin and Stephen K. Merman, *Sound Advice for Job and Career Strategists* (Denver, Colorado: Portland Management Group, 1977), Personal Plan of Action, Part Six, Section Four.

SECTION A
JOB LEAD DEVELOPMENT LETTERS

A-1 COVER LETTER WITH RESUME

Consumer Goods/Services Industries

_____

_____

_____

Dear _____:

    Regarding recent news releases indicating your plans for expansion into the manufacturing of decorative home furnishings, I feel that you will be interested in the experience I have in this specialty.

    As Sales Manager for a small midwest manufacturer of decorative home furnishings, sales were increased over 200%.

    In addition to our own sales force of fifteen, I added a dealer and manufacturer's representative organization to expand sales to two additional regions.

    Further, I was instrumental in implementing procedures to continually monitor retail sales projections. This resulted in a 15% reduction in inventory.

    Although you may not be currently considering additional staffing, I would still appreciate the opportunity to meet with you and discuss future possibilities. My resume is enclosed for your review.

    I will be in Phoenix next week for the National Trade Show and in Minneapolis from April 20–23. I will contact you to arrange an appointment. I am looking forward to discussing our mutual interests.

    Sincerely Yours,

A-2 COVER LETTER WITH RESUME

Technical Industries

_____

_____

_____

Dear _____:

    Recently, I have noticed your firm's advances in the field of _____. I felt that you may be interested in my background in this area.

Previous to my current position, I was heavily involved in the research and development of support systems that included purchasing and budgeting responsibilities.

I have experience as both a person on the line and as a supervisor in research and development units. I consider myself a technically-oriented professional with management and supervisor skills which produce results.

The attached resume summarizes my background. I plan to be in _____ on the 20th of this month. I will call before leaving to see if we could arrange a time to discuss my potential contribution to your organization.

Sincerely Yours,

A-3 LETTER/RESUME

Consumer Goods/Services Industries

_____

_____

_____

Dear _____:

Assuming that most dynamic organizations such as yours are constantly searching for new and creative talent, I am summarizing my background reflecting a person seeking challenge, opportunity, and a growth experience. Following are some of my accomplishments:

* Created and established a new department that drew strong support both from our organization and the community.

* Recruited, trained, and motivated personnel to accomplish tasks thought impossible. Facilitated their growth into a real team effort.

* Promoted a public relations effort that has been quoted and modeled in several publications.

* Administered the most cost-effective department in our organization and was awarded special consideration at the annual board of directors meeting.

Currently, I am searching for other growth opportunities. I am in hopes that the above accomplishments would be profitable for your organization and would appreciate the opportunity to meet with you at your convenience. I will call later this week to arrange an appointment.

Sincerely Yours,

A-4 LETTER/RESUME

Social Service Fields

Date _____

_____
_____
_____

Dear _____:

From a recent article in the Training and Development Journal, I was impressed by your organization's human resource development program. It appears as a dynamic and worthwhile program for employees and I congratulate your human resource development staff for their creative thinking.

Your particular approach is congruent to my own background and philosophy. Assuming that you may be looking for personnel who could significantly maintain your program, I am summarizing my background and experience. I believe that the following experiences and accomplishments reflect the type of individual you are seeking:

* Winner of a National Award for innovative training and development programs.
* Responsible for the design and implementation of an executive development program for my organization.
* Graduate of one of the original degree programs in human resource development. (State University, 1974).
* Over eight years experience as a teacher and small group facilitator.
* Considerable skill in human relations and in solving communication problems within organizations.
* Consulted extensively with companies in the United States and in foreign countries in the design and implementation of career planning programs.
* Consistent, dynamic and enthusiastic involvement in community affairs.
* Married with four children and an actively involved family.

I would appreciate the opportunity to elaborate on these accomplishments and to determine where I may be of value to your organization.

I plan to attend the national convention in _____

during February of next year. I am familiar with the program you are presenting and would like to meet with you at that time. As the convention nears, I will contact you for a specific time and place.

Sincerely,

A-5 ACTION LETTER

Accomplishments/Benefits

Date _____

_____

_____

_____

Dear _____;

In the recent edition of Apartment and Construction News, your firm was featured as an innovative designer of shopping centers.

I would be very interested in the growth opportunities such an organization as yours would provide.

Since my philosophies in exterior design seem very compatible to yours, you may be interested in my qualifications. As shopping centers have significant appeal to women, I feel that as a young woman involved in the marketplace, I can provide a variety of dynamic and creative ideas for your organization.

Some of my accomplishments are:

* Recently completed the design concept for a $6 million shopping complex designed for high quality specialty shops.
* Received the Mart Award for Design Excellence for the innovative design of an indoor recreational complex.

Your organization would certainly provide the challenge and creative stimulation I have found to be central to my career.

I will be in Atlanta on June 6 and would very much like to share some of my ideas with you. I will call prior to that visit to confirm a time and place.

Sincerely,

A-6 ACTION LETTER

Problem Solver

Date _____

_____
_____
_____

Dear _____:

Recently, I have become active in the solar energy field and am writing this letter to summarize my contributions to that growing and dynamic industry.

As a staff member at the _____ Company, I was closely involved with design and development of the solar collector. One of the major problems confronting our staff was the economical methods employed to create a useful, long-lasting design.

Through careful analysis of properties of materials, I was able to correct a material deficiency and thus cut the cost of the collector by some 25%.

In addition, I was able to determine a cost/effective system in producing the casing and generator design unit.

My enthusiastic interest in solar energy not only stems from an engineering and technical background but also from a concerned citizen in regards to the current energy crisis.

I am a creative problem solver and could offer your growing and creative organization several cost effective, profit producing ideas.

I plan to attend the opening of the Solar Energy Research Center in June and noticed that you will also be attending. Perhaps I can meet you and arrange a more formal discussion of our mutual concerns.

Sincerely,

A-7 ACTION LETTER

Alumni

Date _____

_____

_____

_____

Dear _____:

     Recently, I have become active in the Alumni Association for State University. I noticed that you are also a member of the Alumni Association in your area.

     My family and I plan to relocate in _____ and I would like to transfer my affiliation prior to our relocation. I am interested in the alumni activities of your area and would like to receive the newsletter. In addition, I am seeking information as to career and job opportunities in your city.

     I plan to visit your city in March of this year and would appreciate the opportunity to meet with you and your association. Please call me collect at (219) 577-9002 at your earliest convenience so that we may arrange an interview.

     Sincerely Yours,

A-8 ACTION LETTER

Congratulations to Recently Promoted

Date _____

_____

_____

_____

Dear _____:

     Enclosed is a copy of the news article announcing your recent promotion. I offer my congratulations and wish you continued success at _____. I have closely followed your organization and feel confident that your appointment as _____ will have significant impact.

     One of your priorities, I'm sure, is to assess your new staff to determine if any changes or additions are needed.

     I am confidentially exploring new opportunities and will be forwarding, under separate cover, a summary of my qualifications.

     Again, congratulations and best wishes.

     Sincerely,

A-9 ACTION LETTER

Congratulations to Recently Promoted via Third Party

Date _____

_____
_____
_____

Dear _____:

Recently, I learned through a mutual friend, Bill Smith, that you have accepted a new position with _____. Bill suggested that I contact you to confidentially discuss my present situation.

He felt that you would be assessing your staff to determine if any changes or additions were needed.

I have enclosed a short resume for you to review and will contact you in several days for an appointment to determine if there is mutual interest.

Congratulations and best wishes for continued success.

Very Truly Yours,

A-10 EMPLOYMENT AGENCY COVER LETTER AND RESUME

Date _____

_____
_____
_____

Dear _____:

I am confidentially exploring new opportunities in _____ and felt you might be interested in my experience and background:

I am willing to relocate (preferably _____), presently earning $18,600 annually and will be available for interviews between June 1st and 15th. However, if you should have some leads before then, I could make arrangements with proper notice.

Since I am just beginning to explore new situations, I am concerned with the confidential aspect of this job search. I'm hoping that you will be of some assistance.

I will call you next Thursday afternoon to answer any questions you may have or arrange an interview.

Sincerely,

A-11 SEARCH FIRM COVER LETTER AND RESUME

Date _____

_____

_____

_____

Dear _____,

Over the next several months, I will be making some very difficult decisions concerning my career growth with my present employer.

I am interested in confidentially exploring new opportunities and have enclosed two copies of my resume for your personal review.

My own experience has included both line and staff responsibilities and I am currently Assistant to the Vice President of Operations for

_____.

The enclosed summary reflects my skills and abilities. I am currently earning $ _____ plus benefits.

I am open to discussing any situations you may currently have or may have in the near future. Please feel free to contact me at anytime.

Sincerely,

A-12 AD RESPONSE LETTER WITH RESUME

Date _____

_____

_____

_____

Dear _____:

Regarding your recent advertisement in the Daily Post, I am confident you can use a person with the following qualifications:

* Ability to create and implement cost effective programs.
* Skill to coordinate and maintain tight control over a number of projects at one time.
* Ability to work efficiently and effectively with people.
* Ability to solve problems with meaningful and creative solutions.

My resume is enclosed summarizing where these skills and abilities were developed. I would like to utilize them to increase efficiency and profit for your organization.

I will call in a few days to arrange an interview.

Sincerely,

A-13 AD RESPONSE—BLIND BOX

Third Party Confidential

Date _____

Box B-100

New York, N.Y.

Gentlemen:

As a result of the exciting opportunity described in your recent advertisement for _____. I have been asked to respond on behalf of a business associate who would appear to be well-qualified for the position. Because of his position and visibility in the business community, his need for confidentiality is understandable.

His recent accomplishments include:

* Expansion into international markets.
* Successful positioning of two new products resulting in immediate market penetration.
* Instrumental in increasing company sales volume by $150 million.

My associate would very much like to explore this opportunity and is requesting additional information, primarily a job description, location and name of the company and general compensation range prior to submitting his resume for your review.

Thank you for understanding the need for confidentiality.

Sincerely,

A-14 AD RESPONSE—BLIND BOX

Total Confidentiality

Date _____

Box A-1009

Boston, Mass.

Gentlemen:

The exciting opportunity described in your recent advertisement has sparked my imagination and has motivated me to consider changing from my present organization.

I would bring to your organization considerable experience for the position you describe. My most recent accomplishment was a successful reorganization and streamlining of operations resulting in a 16% reduction in overall costs. Sales for the last two years are up 250% with a considerable increase in net profit.

I would respond openly to your advertisement; however, my organization would not treat this matter lightly should they discover my intentions. As a result of this need for total confidentiality, I would appreciate additional information and the identity of your organization. Please respond to P.O. Box B-19, Detroit, Michigan.

Thank you for understanding the need for confidentiality.

Sincerely,

A-15 LETTER TO PROFESSIONAL ASSOCIATION OFFICER

Date _____

_____

_____

_____

Dear _____:

As Executive Director of _____, you may come in contact with corporate situations in which I may be interested. Your knowledge of companies and current industry trends would prove to be of valuable assistance in my current search for a solid career opportunity.

Enclosed is a summary of my qualifications for your personal review.

I would appreciate a few minutes of your time to hear your advice. I will call you in a few days to arrange for an appointment. Thank you in advance for your consideration.

Sincerely,

A-16 LETTER TO CONFERENCE ATTENDEES

Date _____

_____

_____

_____

Dear _____:

I understand that you plan to attend the National Conference in June of this year. As a representative of one of the more unique and fast-growing organizations in our industry, I am sure you will provide a significant contribution to the program.

I am also attending the conference and was fortunate in being invited as a session presenter. I cordially invite you to attend this session and hear my ideas on _____. Also, I feel I could gain considerable insight from your experiences in this area.

I would like the opportunity to meet with you sometime during the conference to discuss our mutual interests in this career field.

I will contact you upon my arrival at the convention to arrange a time.

Until then, best wishes to continued growth and I'll see you in _____.

Sincerely,

A-17 LETTER TO REFERENCES WITH RESUME

Date _____

_____

_____

_____

Dear _____:

As you may or may not know, I am seeking new growth opportunities in _____ and would appreciate your help as a reference.

Since I have not seen you recently, I have enclosed a resume updating my activities. Should you hear of any opportunities, I would appreciate your letting me know.

If a job lead develops to the point of "reference checking," I will fill you in on the position prior to anyone contacting you.

My sincere appreciation for your help and cooperation.

Sincerely,

SECTION B
GENERAL THANK YOU FOR
INFORMATION AND INTERVIEW
FOLLOW-UP LETTERS

B-1 GENERAL THANK YOU FOR INFORMATION

Date _____

_____

_____

_____

Dear _____:

Just a short note of appreciation for the time you spent with me on the telephone earlier this week.

On your suggestion, I contacted _____ and although s/he did not have anything too promising at this time, I was referred to another company with several opportunities.

Again, thank you for your interest. You don't know what it means to a job-seeker to hear a friendly voice on the telephone.

Best personal regards,

B-2 SECRETARY THANK YOU

Date _____

_____

_____

_____

Dear _____:

I would like to express my appreciation for your taking time to fill me in one the new developments at _____.

Mr./Ms. _____and I had a profitable time together. Your comments prompted me to discuss several things in my background that may be of assistance to your organization.

Your help was warmly accepted and appreciated and I hope to see you again.

Cordially,

B-3 ASSOCIATION THANK YOU

Date _____

_____

_____

_____

Dear _____:

     I appreciate the information you forwarded and the current mailing list of the association's members and local chapters.

     I wasn't aware until reading the literature that there are so many opportunities available in _____. I certainly will thoroughly investigate your city as a possible relocation site.

     I have taken the liberty of enclosing a copy of my resume. Please feel free to pass any applicable information to anyone you personally feel may be interested.

     Again, thank you for your assistance.

     Sincerely,

B-4 FIRST INTERVIEW FOLLOW-UP

Date _____

_____

_____

_____

Dear _____,

     Regarding our discussion on May 15, I would like to express my sincere appreciation for your time. I found our interview both rewarding and informative. Your organization appears dynamic and growing.

     I wish you continued success and trust I will have the opportunity of meeting you again.

     Sincerely,

B-5 FINAL INTERVIEW FOLLOW-UP

Date _____

_____

_____

_____

Dear _____,

    Our final meeting on June 7 confirmed my commitment to join your organization. I am impressed by the opportunity and growth offered by your organization, particularly the opportunity to design and develop the plans for _____.

    I hope I am extended an opportunity to demonstrate that I can make a contribution to your organization.

    Sincerely,

B-6 MAILGRAM FOLLOW-UP

MY VISIT YESTERDAY PROVED TO BE A REWARDING AND EYE-OPENING EXPERIENCE. I NEVER REALIZED THE POTENTIAL THAT YOUR FIRM HAS. I WOULD ENJOY A SECOND OPPORTUNITY TO MEET YOUR DYNAMIC STAFF AS I HAVE ADDITIONAL IDEAS TO SHARE.
    THANK YOU.

B-7 TELEGRAM FOLLOW-UP

I HAVE THOROUGHLY ENJOYED THESE INTERVIEW SESSIONS...I FEEL THAT YOUR COMPANY WOULD OFFER AN EXCITING CHALLENGE. I HOPE I HAVE THE OPPORTUNITY TO PROVE THAT I CAN DO THE JOB.
    THANK YOU.

(Note: Generally, a telegram should be used only following a final interview for a position. There are, however, instances where a creative use of the telegram would uncover job leads. These instances may include business situations such as notable successes, friends' promotions, or unique business deals, and so on.)

B-8 CENTER OF INFLUENCE FOLLOW-UP

Date _____

_____

_____

Dear _____:

I thought you might like to know that I have accepted a position with _____ and will begin next week.

I was referred to my new company by _____, whose name you gave me.

Since I will be working close to your office building, I would like to take you to lunch soon to personally thank you for all your help.

I'll call to arrange a time.

Best Regards,

SECTION C
CREATING AND MAINTAINING CENTERS
OF INFLUENCE

C-1 NEW RESPONSIBILITY/PROMOTION—WITHIN AN ORGANIZATION

Date _____

_____
_____
_____

Dear _____:

    May I add my congratulations in your recent promotion with _____.

    I have closely followed your organization's growth during the past years and am confident that you will provide the continued leadership necessary to meet the long-range objectives.

    Again, my sincere congratulations.

    Sincerely,

C-2 NEW POSITION—ARTICLE IN NEWSPAPER OR PERIODICAL

Date _____

_____
_____
_____

Dear _____:

    Your new assignment was recently announced in the Wall Street Journal. I offer my sincere congratulations and wish you much success.

    I have closely followed your organization for some time and am confident that your appointment will contribute significantly to growth and prosperity.

    Since the article mentioned that you would be seeking new directions, I'm sure your first order of business is reassessing staff needs.

    I am currently exploring new opportunities and will be forwarding under separate cover, a summary of my qualifications.

    Again, congratulations and best wishes with your new position.

    Sincerely,

C-3 ACKNOWLEDGMENT OF AN ORGANIZATIONAL PRESS RELEASE

Date _____

_____

_____

_____

Dear _____,

From a recent news release in the Daily Post, your organization appears to be one that is in touch with the current problems confronting our industry. An organization such as yours needs creative and unique talent to provide the necessary leadership to maximize profits and cut costs.

I am enclosing the following summary of my background as the type of person that would best fit your dynamic and far-reaching organizational goals:

* I was instrumental in reducing man-power needs some 15%.

* I am a creative problem solver with an ever-increasing desire to make organizations more efficient and effective.

* I can document instances where different units of an organization were coordinated under my supervision to create a true team effort for problem solving.

The enclosed resume lists my accomplishments and achievements. Regardless of any openings, I would still welcome the opportunity to meet with you to discuss our mutual interests and concerns in

_____.

Sincerely,

C-4 POSITIVE TURNDOWN OF A JOB OFFER

Date _____

_____

_____

_____

Dear _____,

During my job-search, I interviewed several dynamic and growing organizations. These organizations would provide the maximum growth opportunity both in my personal and professional life. Your organization is no exception. I find your staff to be highly professional, your organization competent and growing and your potential unmatched. Making a decision among these organizations was difficult.

At this time, I have decided to join another organization whose program seems to best fit my current professional, personal, and social goals.

I thoroughly enjoyed meeting you and learning more about your dynamic organization.

I will be in touch with you periodically to share ideas and keep you abreast of my progress at _____.

Again, thank you for your time and consideration.

Yours very truly,

C-5 LETTER REQUESTING A CAREER INFORMATION INTERVIEW (CIIT)

Date _____

_____

_____

_____

Dear _____,

Currently, I am involved in researching information regarding the career of _____. I understand that you are a person in close contact with this field and could provide helpful insight as to its character.

I would greatly appreciate spending a few moments of your time to seek advice concerning this fast-growing and dynamic career field.

I will contact you shortly to arrange an interview.

Thank you for your consideration.

Sincerely,

SECTION FOUR
CORPORATE/ORGANIZATIONAL
RESEARCH PROCESS LETTERS

D-1 ANNUAL REPORT REQUEST

Date _____

_____

_____

_____

Dear _____,

    Currently, I am active in researching potential career opportunities. I have been impressed by your organization's growth potential.

    I would appreciate your forwarding your latest annual report and any quarterly reports you may have available.

    In addition, should you have any pertinent information that may assist me in this research, or would help me be better acquainted with your organization, please forward it as soon as possible.

    Thank you for your cooperation.

    Sincerely,

D-2 CHAMBER OF COMMERCE
INFORMATION REQUEST LETTER

Date _____

_____

_____

_____

Dear _____,

    Your city has always fascinated me and I am currently planning to relocate.

    I would appreciate any assistance you could provide in the way of employer listings, industrial guides, SMSA statistics, and general "newcomers" information.

    Thank you for your cooperation.

    Sincerely,

D-3 REQUEST FOR NEWCOMERS PACKET
FROM MAJOR REAL ESTATE COMPANIES
OR BANKS

Date _____

_____

_____

_____

Dear _____,

Congratulations! Your city has been selected as a place I would like to live. In planning for my relocation, I need your assistance.

Please foward my "newcomers" information or other material you feel would benefit my understanding of the commerce and industry of your city.

Thank you for your cooperation.

Sincerely,

D-4 REQUEST FOR AREA INDUSTRIAL
STATISTICS FROM BANKS

Date _____

_____

_____

_____

Dear _____,

Your bank has been recommended as one that takes a real interest in the community and tries to serve its customers well.

Although I am not yet a customer, I am planning to relocate in _____ and need your assistance in forwarding any documents or sources that would reveal industrial trends or statistics for your area.

Your cooperation in this effort is greatly appreciated.

Sincerely,

Index